Learning Unreal® Engine iOS Game Development

Create exciting iOS games with the power of the new Unreal® Engine 4 subsystems

Muhammad A.Moniem

PUBLISHING

BIRMINGHAM - MUMBAI

Learning Unreal® Engine iOS Game Development

First published: February 2015

Production reference: 1230215

Published by Packt Publishing Ltd.
Livery Place
35 Livery Street
Birmingham B3 2PB, UK.

ISBN 978-1-78439-771-5

www.packtpub.com

Credits

Author
Muhammad A.Moniem

Reviewers
Alankar Pradhan
Mohit Ramani
Sahil Ramani
Sourav Tosh

Commissioning Editor
Edward Bowkett

Acquisition Editors
Rebecca Youé
Richard Gall

Content Development Editor
Arwa Manasawala

Technical Editor
Faisal Siddiqui

Copy Editors
Pranjali Chury
Brinda S. Madhu

Project Coordinator
Purav Motiwalla

Proofreaders
Simran Bhogal
Stephen Copestake
Paul Hindle
Bernadette Watkins

Indexer
Mariammal Chettiyar

Production Coordinator
Manu Joseph

Cover Work
Manu Joseph

About the Author

Muhammad A.Moniem started in the industry at a very early age. He taught himself everything related to the game development process even before he joined college. After being a software engineer, he started to teach himself the art of game design and game art techniques. As a self-taught person, he was able to find his way into the industry very easily, which led him to be hired for big, medium, and small companies, titles, and teams. Throughout his career, he was able to contribute as a full-time or part-time employee, or freelancer on games for a wide range of platforms, including Windows, Mac, iOS, Android, PS4, XBOXOne, and OUYA; he has also worked with technologies such as VR, AR, or Kinect. Finally, he was able to establish his own one-person game company/team as a part-time independent developer. Lots of his indie games got recognition or have been finalists in international indie game events such as IGF, Indie Showcase, IGC, and Tokyo Game Show. He has also designed an amazing website, www.mamoniem.com.

Acknowledgements

I would like to thank all those who helped me make this book possible. A special mention to all the team members at Epic Games for their hard work on Unreal® Engine and for the great decision of making the engine available to everyone by sharing the source code. Without their hard work and tough decisions, this book would not exist. I would like to thank them for their support along the way since I started using Unreal®, and all the people I knew at Epic were supportive and interested in my activities with the engine.

I would like to thank all the people at Packt Publishing who worked on this book. They helped me a lot and were patient when I got out of my schedule because of my personal obligations. A special thanks to the technical reviewers; they constantly checked my errors and omissions. This book has become better because of them; thanks to all their hard work. Richard, Arwa, Rebecca, and Faisal; thank you for bringing me on board at Packt and helping me put the book together.

Last but not least, I want to express my pleasure of having Lamiaa, Yusuf, and Mariam in my life. You are all my gifts. You are a very supportive family; thanks for giving me the best environment to write this book, and thanks for believing in all my projects. Father and mother, thanks for teaching me how to learn on my own; it helped me a lot to learn and pass on the knowledge.

About the Reviewers

Alankar Pradhan is from Mumbai, Maharashtra, and did his schooling at I.E.S.'s CPV high school. He is an ambitious person who loves interacting with new people, traveling, spending leisure time with friends, or playing games over PC and mobile. Games have always been a passion in his life. More than just playing games, how things work was his main curiosity. Hence, he decided to pursue his career in the same field. He graduated with a BSc in software development from Sheffield Hallam University, UK. He did his master's in game programming (BAC+5 equivalent) from DSK Supinfogame, where he undertook industry-oriented projects to increase his skill set and gave his best to do so. He worked as a game programming intern at The Walt Disney Company India Pvt Ltd. During his internship, he worked on a live project called *Hitout Heroes*, where he was responsible for the integration of small gameplay modules and the social integration of Facebook into the game. Later, the whole UI implementation, working, flow, and mechanism was managed solely by him. At the end, he was responsible for bug solving and memory management. His name was added in the credits due to the noticeable work accomplished. He also interned as a game programmer with DSK Green Ice Games and is currently working as a video game programmer on a game targeted at PCs and consoles.

He has worked on many small projects in teams as well as individually, sharpening his own skills in various languages, such as C#, C++, Java, Unreal® Script, Python, Lua, Groovy/Grails, and HTML5/CSS. He is familiar with engines such as Unity3D, Unreal® Development Kit, Visual Studio and SDKs such as NetBeans, Eclipse, and Wintermute. In 2013, his dissertation on *Comparison between Python and Lua in Gaming Industry* got published as a book. He has previously worked as a technical reviewer on a book called *Creating E-Learning Games With Unity* by *Packt Publishing*.

Besides this, he even likes to read, listen to music, and write poems and short stories at times. He has his own website (http://alan.poetrycraze.com) where he posts his poems and has also published a book called *The Art Of Lost Words, CreateSpace Independent Publishing Platform*, which is available at www.amazon.com.

E-mail: alankar.pradhan@gmail.com
Portfolio site: alankarpradhan.wix.com/my-portfolio
Social: www.facebook.com/alankar.pradhan

We are so often caught up in our aim that we forget to appreciate the journey; especially the people we meet on the way. Appreciation is a wonderful feeling; its way better if we don't overlook it. I hereby like to take this opportunity to acknowledge the people who directed me and inspired me in this initiative.

I would like to express my heartily thanks to my parents, who instilled me and always believed in me. I am also thankful to my friends for their constant support and encouraging words that helped me to reach this level.

Last but not the least, I would like to thank all the people who are directly or indirectly involved in this and helped me.

Mohit Ramani is an engineering graduate from Bharati Vidyapeeth, Pune. He graduated in 2010 and went on to work with some of the major game development companies before starting his own gaming venture in 2013. He has hands-on experience in development of games on Android, iOS, Web, Windows, and consoles and has more than 25 titles under his belt, including major titles on PS2, PSP, PS3, and PC.

He now runs his own gaming company in New Delhi—Digital Agents Interactive Private Limited—where they develop games and interactive solutions for mobiles, PCs, and consoles. They also use technologies such as augmented and virtual reality in their projects to make them more immersive and engaging. Their aim is to be the most innovative gaming company in India.

Personal website: www.mohitramani.com
Facebook: https://www.facebook.com/mohit.ramani
Company website: www.digitalagents.in

I would like to thank my parents, Hardayal Kewal Ramani and Madhu Kewal Ramani, my two brothers, Vishal Ramani and Mukul Ramani, my cousin and partner, Dalip Kewalramani, my friends, and last but not least, my team at Digital Agents Interactive without whose support, it would not have been possible for me to reach this stage and review this book. I thank them all for being there when I needed them.

Sahil Ramani is an avid graphics and game developer with a master's degree in game development and has experience working in both animation and game studios. His varied experience includes building game engines, tools, and frameworks for personal and professional gain. Among the free game engines available online, he has experience working with Unity 3D, Unreal® Engine, and OGRE in order to build games for Windows, Linux, and MacOSX, apart from iOS and Android.

I would like to thank Packt Publishing for giving me the opportunity to review this book on such a niche topic, and I wish the author the best in his future endeavors.

Sourav Tosh is a software engineer currently working for Electronic Arts. Driven by an early interest in games and programming, he would often write small games and demos and show them to his friends and family. He has worked on titles for PC, consoles, and mobile devices. He has previously worked for Lakshya Digital and Trine Games Studio. He has worked with a number of commercial game engines, including Infernal Engine, Esenthel Engine, Unreal® Engine, and Unity3D Engine. While not reading games programming books or making games, he enjoys playing video games and board games.

I am particularly grateful to my teacher, Amal Kanti Seal, without whom, I probably would not have developed an interest in programming in the first place, and my closest friend, Anindya Raychaudhuri, who spends hours and hours working with me on games and keeping the dream alive. It was, in fact, his computer where I discovered the magical world of video games. A heartfelt thanks also goes to my love, Sampita Tosh, who always believed in me and encouraged me to go forward. Without her sacrifices, this would never have been possible.

www.PacktPub.com

Support files, eBooks, discount offers, and more

For support files and downloads related to your book, please visit www.PacktPub.com.

Did you know that Packt offers eBook versions of every book published, with PDF and ePub files available? You can upgrade to the eBook version at www.PacktPub.com and as a print book customer, you are entitled to a discount on the eBook copy. Get in touch with us at service@packtpub.com for more details.

At www.PacktPub.com, you can also read a collection of free technical articles, sign up for a range of free newsletters and receive exclusive discounts and offers on Packt books and eBooks.

http://PacktLib.PacktPub.com

Do you need instant solutions to your IT questions? PacktLib is Packt's online digital book library. Here, you can search, access, and read Packt's entire library of books.

Why subscribe?

- Fully searchable across every book published by Packt
- Copy and paste, print, and bookmark content
- On demand and accessible via a web browser

Free access for Packt account holders

If you have an account with Packt at www.PacktPub.com, you can use this to access PacktLib today and view 9 entirely free books. Simply use your login credentials for immediate access.

Table of Contents

Preface   **1**

Chapter 1: Prepare to Make Unreal Games with
Unreal® Engine – Installing and Setting Up   **7**

  Getting ready and setting up   **8**
    What if I don't have a Mac OS computer?   8
  Getting and building the engine   **9**
    Direct download   9
    GitHub version   11
  Preparing the other required tools   **15**
    XCode 5.1 or higher   15
    3D and 2D applications   15
    The application loader   16
    iTunes and iTools   16
  Preparing a game profile on the App Store   **16**
    Generating certificates   18
    Generating an App ID   20
  Adding devices   **20**
  Generating provisioning profiles   **21**
  Summary   **23**

Chapter 2: Methods and Tools to Create Your Games   **25**
  Blueprints inside Unreal® Engine   **25**
    Different types of blueprints   27
  The need for blueprints   **28**
  What is a node?   **29**
  The iOS/Mobile-only nodes   **30**

Blueprints – tips and tricks	**37**
The iOS project pipeline	**39**
Building the game's provisioning profiles	**39**
Setting up the game's provisioning profile	39
Creating a new project	40
Editing the project settings	41
Editing the *.plist file	45
Building a project	**45**
Launching	46
Packaging	46
Summary	**48**
Chapter 3: Creating a Brick Breaking Game	**49**
The project structure	**50**
Building the blueprints	**50**
Gameplay mechanics	51
Starting a new level	51
Building the game mode	**52**
Building the game's main material	**53**
Building the blueprints and components	55
Building the layout blueprint	56
Building the ball blueprint	60
Building the platform blueprint	63
Building the graphs and logic	63
The layout blueprint graph	66
The Ball blueprint graph	70
The platform blueprint graph	72
Summary	**76**
Chapter 4: Advanced Game Content Generation with a Fruit Chopper Game	**77**
The project structure	**78**
Importing the assets	**78**
An overview of blueprints	**80**
The gameplay mechanic	**81**
The game levels	82
Building the particles	**82**
Building the material	82
Building the particle system	84
Building the blueprints	**85**
Player controller	85
Fruits blueprints	86

Bomb blueprint 90
Win/lose blueprints 91
LevelLogic fruitsGame blueprint 92
Summary **100**
Chapter 5: Building an Exciting Endless Runner Game **101**
The project structure **102**
Importing the assets **102**
Building the animated sprites **103**
An overview of blueprints **105**
The gameplay mechanics **105**
Building the blueprints **106**
Building the logic **110**
Pushing the boundaries **116**
Summary **117**
Chapter 6: Designing an Advanced Game **119**
The project structure **119**
Importing the assets **120**
Building the animated sprites **120**
The blueprints **121**
The gameplay mechanic **122**
Building the blueprints **123**
gameInputs 123
uiText 126
mainChar 126
enemyRed 128
crateBox 130
bullet 130
shootingFGameMode 131
spawnPoint 131
Building the logic **131**
uiText 132
enemyRed 133
spawnPoint 134
bullet 136
mainChar 137
Using 2D colliders **140**
Pushing the boundaries **142**
Summary **142**

Chapter 7: Monetizing Your Game	**143**
iAd support	144
iTunes Connect	145
Adding in-app purchases	148
Adding leaderboards	149
Adding achievements	151
Summary	153
Chapter 8: iOS Debugging and Optimization	**155**
Blueprints Live view	155
Printing messages	157
Breakpoints	159
XCode tools	164
Debug Navigator	165
Capturing frames	168
Instruments	169
Performance optimization	170
Minimizing the game size	170
Summary	171
Chapter 9: Publishing	**173**
Packaging the project	173
Editing the game profile	179
Uploading and submiting for review	180
Summary	186
Appendix: Nodes Database	**187**
Index	**191**

Preface

This book is meant to help you going into the process of creating an iOS game from scratch using one of the best and oldest engines in the industry—Unreal® Engine 4.

Although the engine was made from the beginning to make AAA games for PC and console, it has recently acquired the market of casual and mobile games with lots of power and creative tools.

During the course of this book, we will go in depth into how to make several casual game types that look a lot like the top selling and profiting games on the App Store.

What will be covered?

Chapter 1, Prepare to Make Unreal Games with Unreal® Engine – Installing and Setting Up, will take you through the process of preparing your environment to develop an iOS game using Unreal® Engine 4. At the end of the day, making an iOS game is completely different from making any other game, even if from other mobile devices.

Chapter 2, Methods and Tools to Create Your Games, discusses the different ways in which we can make a game using Epic's technology, what is the best, and why.

Chapter 3, Creating a Brick Breaking Game, contains the first game to be made in this book. Physics is one of the most important topics in any game engine, so in this chapter, will be making a game based on physics to understand how it works in Unreal® Engine.

Chapter 4, Advanced Game Content Generation with a Fruit Chopper Game, is the second game project in this book and will feature how to make a simple 3D game, which has more animations, effects, and complex swipe inputs.

Chapter 5, Building an Exciting Endless Runner Game, admits that the most famous genre in mobile games in the last few years was the endless runner games. So, we will be taking the ride of making a runner game with a randomly generated level.

Chapter 6, Designing an Advanced Game, tells you what a game is without enemies. All the past examples were based on scoring with some obstacles, but let's add some enemies in that chapter to interact with, in a simple touch-screen-friendly platformer game.

Chapter 7, Monetizing Your Game, will cover the easiest way to get profit from your free games. There are a few techniques that can be added to any mobile/iOS game to make it bring you money.

Chapter 8, iOS Debugging and Optimization, helps you understand why debugging is considered as a top priority when it comes to mobile devices, the pros of finding and fixing bugs, various debugging tools and techniques, and how to optimize performance.

Chapter 9, Publishing, will take you through the process of building and submitting the game to the store review because a game is not a game without an audience. This chapter is the final destination for any game release.

Appendix, Nodes Database, gives you a full database with explanation for each node we have used during the process of making all the four game examples. It will be helpful for you to start improvising and making your own unique games.

Who this book is for

If you are looking for a book that teaches you the game design of a top selling iOS game, then this is the wrong book to read. If you are looking for a book to help you to prepare you art assets and make animations for your games, again this is the wrong book.

This book is mainly focused on the implantation of any art asset that you will use into the engine and how you can start putting everything together; building blueprints; gameplay logic; adding lots of fun, eye candy, and ear candy to the games; and building those games for testing and publishing on the App Store.

If you are a programmer who wants to switch to Unreal® Engine, or a programmer who is willing to learn the visual scripting, or even just a guy who wants to start making games; this is the correct place for you. The book is friendly with everyone who wants to make iOS games using Epic's technology regardless of their background.

What you need for this book

You will need to have a Mac computer (windows PC is fine if you cannot provide a Mac). Also, you will need to have Unreal® Engine (I used 4.3.0 while writing the book), you will need to have XCode (5.1 or later, it depends on your Engine version), And finally a big cup of tea…

Also you need to have a base knowledge of the Mac OSX, as there will be some steps related to the OS itself, so you need to be a bit familiar with it.

Conventions

In this book, you will find a number of styles of text that distinguish between different kinds of information. Here are some examples of these styles, and an explanation of their meaning.

Code words in text, database table names, folder names, filenames, file extensions, pathnames, dummy URLs, user input, and Twitter handles are shown as follows: "We can include other contexts through the use of the `include` directive."

A block of code is set as follows:

```
[default]
exten => s,1,Dial(Zap/1|30)
exten => s,2,Voicemail(u100)
exten => s,102,Voicemail(b100)
exten => i,1,Voicemail(s0)
```

When we wish to draw your attention to a particular part of a code block, the relevant lines or items are set in bold:

```
[default]
exten => s,1,Dial(Zap/1|30)
exten => s,2,Voicemail(u100)
exten => s,102,Voicemail(b100)
exten => i,1,Voicemail(s0)
```

Any command-line input or output is written as follows:

```
# cp /usr/src/asterisk-addons/configs/cdr_mysql.conf.sample
    /etc/asterisk/cdr_mysql.conf
```

New terms and **important words** are shown in bold. Words that you see on the screen, in menus or dialog boxes for example, appear in the text like this: "clicking on the **Next** button moves you to the next screen."

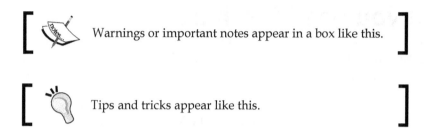

Warnings or important notes appear in a box like this.

Tips and tricks appear like this.

Reader feedback

Feedback from our readers is always welcome. Let us know what you think about this book—what you liked or disliked. Reader feedback is important for us as it helps us develop titles that you will really get the most out of.

To send us general feedback, simply e-mail feedback@packtpub.com, and mention the book's title in the subject of your message.

If there is a topic that you have expertise in and you are interested in either writing or contributing to a book, see our author guide at www.packtpub.com/authors.

Customer support

Now that you are the proud owner of a Packt book, we have a number of things to help you to get the most from your purchase.

Downloading the example code

You can download the example code files from your account at http://www.packtpub.com for all the Packt Publishing books you have purchased. If you purchased this book elsewhere, you can visit http://www.packtpub.com/support and register to have the files e-mailed directly to you.

Errata

Although we have taken every care to ensure the accuracy of our content, mistakes do happen. If you find a mistake in one of our books—maybe a mistake in the text or the code—we would be grateful if you could report this to us. By doing so, you can save other readers from frustration and help us improve subsequent versions of this book. If you find any errata, please report them by visiting http://www.packtpub.com/submit-errata, selecting your book, clicking on the **Errata Submission Form** link, and entering the details of your errata. Once your errata are verified, your submission will be accepted and the errata will be uploaded to our website or added to any list of existing errata under the Errata section of that title.

To view the previously submitted errata, go to https://www.packtpub.com/books/content/support and enter the name of the book in the search field. The required information will appear under the **Errata** section.

Piracy

Piracy of copyrighted material on the Internet is an ongoing problem across all media. At Packt, we take the protection of our copyright and licenses very seriously. If you come across any illegal copies of our works in any form on the Internet, please provide us with the location address or website name immediately so that we can pursue a remedy.

Please contact us at copyright@packtpub.com with a link to the suspected pirated material.

We appreciate your help in protecting our authors and our ability to bring you valuable content.

Questions

If you have a problem with any aspect of this book, you can contact us at questions@packtpub.com, and we will do our best to address the problem.

1
Prepare to Make Unreal Games with Unreal® Engine – Installing and Setting Up

Making games was always a time consuming process that involved many people who had to keep focusing on building a game engine for at least a year before the game itself, and these custom engines would usually not be used with any other game afterwards. However, with the huge evolution of technology, we started to see lots of new handy engines that allow you to build several game types and save you the time of writing an engine from scratch, giving you a chance to focus on the game itself.

A long time ago, each platform was totally independent, and you were required to use a tool tied to the platform to create your own apps and games. Nowadays, however, with the evolution toward multi-platform development, making games for a platform using another one has become a lot easier—more than easy, in fact!

When it comes to making iOS games, there are a number of factors we have to keep in mind. Unreal Engine 4.0 supports the development of iOS games on Windows. However, later versions (4.3 onwards) support the ability to make, build, and test iOS games from within a Windows-based machine and then import them to your iOS device via some special tools that have been developed by Epic. This gives us a wide range of available scenarios when it comes to making/building iOS games using UE4.

Unreal Engine has been on the market for almost 20 years, and the leading AAA companies have used it to make tons and tons of games for a wide range of platforms. However, recently Epic has moved it to another step, where it is open for everyone in the world with a low price and more platform support. This gives lots of people the chance to start using this technology to achieve what was initially exclusive for AAA companies only.

In this chapter, we'll cover the following topics:

- Getting and installing the engine
- Building the source code on Mac
- The difference between the several engine copies
- Tools required for iOS game development
- Creating game profiles on the Apple Developers Portal

Getting ready and setting up

Despite the relative openness of UE4, I would recommend you use a Mac OS X computer for developing iOS games using Unreal (or any other engine for that matter). It's important as it gives you direct access to XCode, which you will need to use to do the following:

- Debugging your game using its console
- Analyzing the game's performance using its tools (instruments)
- Adding a third party's libraries to the XCode project
- Adding platform-specific code to the game's XCode project

What if I don't have a Mac OS computer?

If you don't have an iMac, Mac Pro, or MacBook Air, there are still other options that you can choose:

- Purchase a Mac mini, which is very cheap and can get the job done. With Epic's new system, you can work and make all your games in a Windows-based computer and then move them to your Mac to build and test with more efficient building tools.

- Install a virtual machine on your Windows-based PC using applications like Virtual Box (this saved me one day when I was not able to get a Mac). In this case, you will have a dual OS on one device.

  Use Virtual Box to turn your PC into a fully functional Mac, but it should be done on your own guarantee!

- Your last choice is to run a normal Windows OS PC; you will be able to follow along 100 percent with this book, except only one part where we will build the engine. This should also be a straightforward process on the Windows platform. However, you can save your time and just download the prebuilt version directly from Epic's website.

Getting and building the engine

The first step is to get the engine running. Using Unreal Engine to build iOS games is a little different than using any other tool or engine out there, as Epic took a brave and awesome step by releasing its entire engine source code to its subscribers. We will see two different ways to get the engine running.

Direct download

Downloading UE4 directly will ensure that you have an already compiled version of the engine. All that you have to do is just start using it. You can get it by following these steps:

1. Access the engine home page.

2. Press the **Get Unreal** button and start filling in all your information to make an account with Epic games. Also, you will need to read the engine license and accept it if it works fine with you.

3. After confirming your e-mail and getting your account running, your dashboard will look different. You will see a confirmation of the successful subscription billing.

4. Then, you will see the other options to download the engine. In the case of direct download, you have to pick the launcher OS version you want: Windows or Mac. In my case, I've picked the Mac version (keep in mind that it will download a launcher, which is approximately 50 MB only).

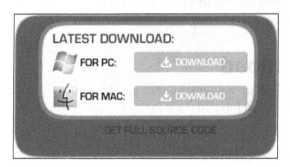

5. When you run the launcher, you will find many useful links to the forums, answer hubs, and marketplace where you can find free projects among other things.

    You can go to the library and select an engine version (the latest should be the best; I'm running 4.3 while writing this book, as it is the latest one and was just released a few days ago) and start installing it. After you finish, you will see a new section called **Engine Slots**, which holds all the engine versions you are running via the launcher.

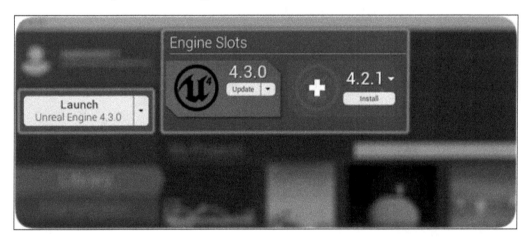

6. Finally, you can run the engine!

GitHub version

The GitHub version is not just a precompiled copy of the engine; it contains the full C++ source code of the engine, which means if you are a ninja coder and you want to add new features or fix the engine bugs and improve it, this is the best way to get your copy. Also, if you are a beginner in the engine world or a student who wants to learn more about the engine constructions, your best bet is to get the GitHub version:

1. After the first three steps in the previous method (opening the engine page and registering an account with Epic), instead of selecting to download a launcher, you will need to access the GitHub version to get the full source code of the engine.

2. Follow the link in the GitHub instructions to access the repository.

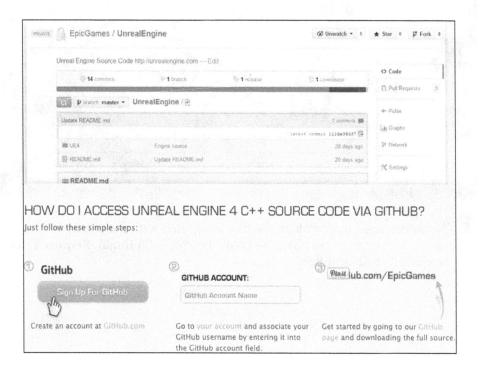

3. To be able to access Epic's repository of the engine in GitHub (which is a private repository), you will need to list your GitHub account name (make a new one if you don't have one already) in your account settings. This should be enough to connect your GitHub account with Epic's GitHub group. If you access your GitHub account, you should now find Epic listed in your organizations list.

4. From the available branches, you can select the version of the engine you want to download, or you can directly access all the release versions from the **release** tag at the top of the page:

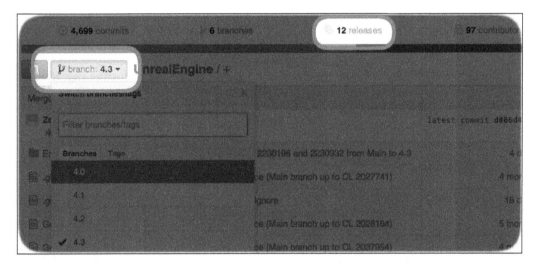

5. Now, you need to download the files associated with the engine version you chose. Ensure that you download only 4 out of 5: **Optional**, **Required_1of2**, **Required_2of2**, and **Source code(zip)**.

6. Now, as we have all the required files, we need to extract all of them while ensuring that the files are together in the same folder, without replacement of any of the folders. As all of the ZIP files contain the same folder names (as they are all related to one dependency), you might need to press *Alt* on your Mac while merging the files/folders and select **Keep Newer** to add them instead of replacing them.

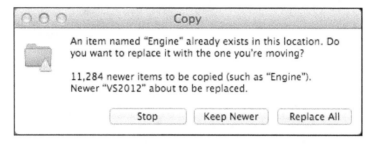

7. After finishing the file merge process, you will end up with the final engine source code files, which is approximately 6.5 GB. All that you need now is to run the script that is responsible for generating the project files. If you are using a Mac, which is our case, then you need to run GenerateProjectFiles.command; otherwise you can run it's Windows equivalent, GenerateProjectFiles.bat.

8. This project file autogenerating process will hold for a few minutes and it will end up adding some files to your engine's folders and directories. However, the only one you can see and the only one you need right now to build the engine will be in the root directory: it will be an XCode project file named UE4.xcodeproj or a Visual Studio solution called UE4.sln on Windows.

9. Run this project in XCode 5.1 or later. Give it a while to index your project, which might take approximately 30 minutes or less, depending on your Mac speed. Don't be in a rush, as it might break everything if you start building to soon. You should wait till the activity viewer bar at the top of XCode finishes indexing and tells you that it is ready.

10. Now, it is time for the final step: building and running the engine. We just need to define what exactly we are going to build. In this case, we want to build an Unreal Engine Editor for Mac. So, we need to open the **Set the active scheme** menu from the top-left corner and select the **UE4Editor – Mac** scheme. Now, you can click on **Build and run**, and this will give you a debug build of the editor that could be a little slow and buggy. If you want a final build that is more optimized, efficient, and free from the debugging code, you could easily build using **Product**, **Build For**, and finally **Profiling**.

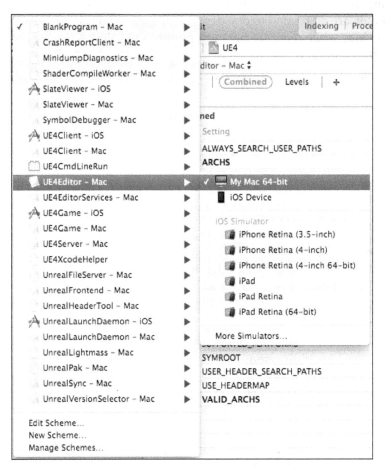

After building, the Unreal Editor will run automatically. Whenever you want to run the Editor, you don't have to build it again; you just need to browse to the build location and open it. The location for Mac and Windows is as follows:

For Mac: `UnrealEngine-4.3.0-release /Engine/Binaries/Mac/ UE4Editor-4.3.0.app`

For Windows: `UnrealEngine-4.3.0-release /Engine/Binaries/Win64/ UE4Editor.exe`

Keep in mind that the final `*.app` name might be different; it depends on the build type you made. Here, I made a debug engine build and my final engine application file was named `Debug.app` by default, which I then changed to `UE4Editor-4.3.0`. Feel free to change it; as long as you have different engine builds running at the same time, you will need to define them to avoid any confusion.

Preparing the other required tools

Making an iOS game with Unreal Engine doesn't mean that we will only be using Unreal Engine throughout the process. During the course of this book, you will need other tools and applications running too. Here are the other tools you will need and why.

XCode 5.1 or higher

As you saw in the previous steps, we used XCode to build our engine because it is the main IDE for Mac OS X. It is an essential tool and we will need it again anytime we want to rebuild the engine or write a C++ game using the generated project from Unreal Engine. As Epic has outlined, for Mac users, the minimum version to be used with Unreal Engine 4.x should be 5.1.

3D and 2D applications

As this book will take care of the process of making games using UE4, it is ultimately down to you whether you choose to use the assets provided with the book or your own that will fit your requirements. If you are going to build your own assets, I would recommend that you use Blender3D for the 3D assets or Inkscape for the 2D assets. I used both of these applications while I was building the examples presented in this book. Both are free/open source applications with high-end quality and tools.

The application loader

When we finish our game, we will need to submit it to Apple for review. The best and the only way to upload *.ipa files to Apple is using the Application Loader app. It is free and easily available. Later in *Chapter 9, Publishing*, you will learn how to use it during the submission process.

iTunes and iTools

If you are running on a Mac, then iTunes will be installed by default. However, if you are running on Windows, you will need to install it, as it is the best way to push an *.ipa installation file to your device to test it. If you cannot get hold of this, you can get iTools, which is very easy and straightforward to install and it runs on Mac and Windows. I used to use both applications all the time to push *.ipa builds to an authorized device outside XCode.E- iOS 6.0.

To be able to run Unreal Engine 4 games, you must have at least an iPhone 4 or iPad 2 running iOS 6.0 or later.

Preparing a game profile on the App Store

As I already mentioned, making an iOS game is a little different than making any other mobile game. For iOS games in particular, there are many steps involved in the preproduction period; these steps should be done first on the App Store developer's portal to be able to run a test on a device.

To be able to run these steps, you must have an Apple iOS developer account; if you don't have one yet, then apply for one. It is a straightforward process, and like purchasing any other account, you will need to provide an Apple account number and a credit card or any other valid online payment method.

Registering for an iOS developer account should be processed quickly, so if you apply as an independent person, you might get the approval within two days. However, if you apply as a company, then it might take up to two weeks or a bit more.

Now, you have an Apple iOS account (your developer account permits you to develop or access the iOS dev center only; you will not be able to access Mac or Safari dev centers). We now have to perform several steps, which should be done in proper order, as some steps will be based on the previous steps. The good thing about the latest updates from Apple is that they made a new and better control panel, which organizes with the correct order. Previously, the control panel was a bit messy, which made it difficult to find what you want.

Generating certificates

Generating a certificate is a process that needs to be started in the development device (your Mac) and then completed in the Apple developer's portal.

First, you will need to open **KeyChain Access**, and through the drop-down menu of **KeyChain Access**, select **Certificate Assistant**. Finally, click on **Request a Certificate from a Certified Authority**.

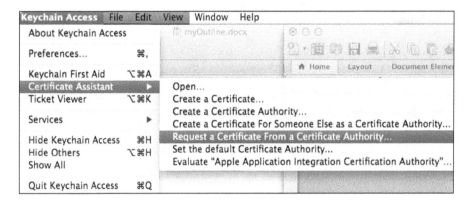

From the **Certificate Assistant** window, fill the **User Email Address** field with your e-mail, insert a common name, and mark the **Save to disk** option to save the file to your disk. Click on **Continue** and save it to your desktop (or somewhere you can remember later).

This process will generate a file with a `*.certSigningRequest` extension. Go directly to the Apple developer's portal, access the iOS developers, and click on the **Certificates** section.

Click on **Add**, and you will be moved to a screen where you need to select a certificate type. Keep in mind that we will use the generated `*.certSigningRequest` extension twice. We will generate a development certificate to be used for the testing phase, and then we will make one for production, which will be used for the final build and store submission version of your games.

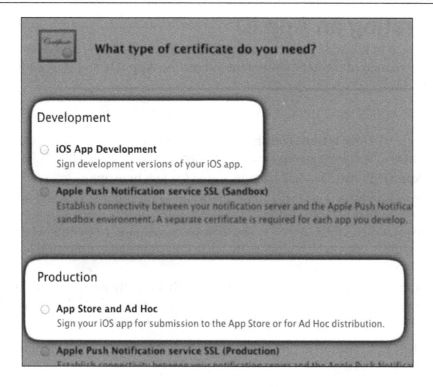

Here, select **iOS App Development** and click on **Continue**. In the following screen, you will find some information about how to make the `*.certSigningRequest` file, which we already made. Then, you can click on **Continue** and select the file from your desktop (or wherever you saved it).

Click on **Generate**, and this will provide you with a valid development certificate; download it.

Redo the same process, but this time, select **App Store and Ad Hoc** and use the same process to generate the production certificate and download it.

Now, as you have two certificates downloaded (files with the `*.cer` extension), double-click on each of them. This will run **KeyChain Access** for you and ask you whether you really want to install it. Do the process twice, as we will require one development certificate while building and testing and another one for the distribution build.

After installing both, you will find that they have a green icon next to each of them, and this tells you that both are valid.

Generating an App ID

Now, go back to the main panel in your iOS developer account screen, and from the section named **Identifiers**, choose the subsection **App IDs** and start adding a new App ID.

The process is very simple and it involves adding some inputs:

- **App ID Description**: You should describe your game/app within a small phrase. Normally, using your game name is enough to fill this input field.
- **App ID Prefix**: This will be auto added for you by Apple.
- **App ID Suffix**: This is the most important input (Bundle ID), and this is the one that will be used in your provisioning profile. Usually, you write the word com followed by . and then your company name followed by another . after which you finally write the game name, for example, com. companyName.GameName.
- **App Services**: This allows you to select what exactly the game will be supporting. Keep in mind that you can come here again and edit the ID and regenerate it, so don't worry if you forget something.

Finally, click on **Continue** to finish the process of adding the App ID (Bundle ID).

Adding devices

As a part of the secure development environment that Apple provides to developers, you can define which devices are authorized to try the game/app during the development process. So, in case someone gets a development version of the game, he/she will not be able to run it on his/her device. Only the devices that are included in the provisioning profile (we will explain how to do this shortly) will be able to run the game build.

Adding a new device is a very simple process; you just hit the **Add new device** button in the **Devices** section on your left panel, and then provide the following details:

- **Name**: This is a name to identify whose device it is. Any name works fine.
- **UDID**: This is the unique identifier of the device. If you don't know how to get this, the easiest way is to simply connect your device to a Mac/PC and open iTunes. You will find the number directly on your device screen.

One last thing regarding the devices. Apple's developer portal allows you to add up to 100 devices in your devices list. These devices will not be per project but per account, meaning that you can have 100 devices as a company only; so, use them wisely if you are working in a huge team! Anyway, an iOS game in any size will not require such a massive team!

Generating provisioning profiles

This is our last and main destination in the process of preparing the game profile in Apple's developer portal, as all the previous steps were made to serve this process. All we need from the developer's portal are the provisioning profile files. With these files, we will be able to make a valid build (either development or release), but to have these valid files, we had to set up the certificate, App ID, and devices; you will see how useful and time saving it is to finish these three things beforehand, just as we did.

Now, in the last section of the developer panel in Apple's developer portal, which is named **Provisioning Profiles**, click to add a new provisioning profile. Then, you will be prompted to four different screens:

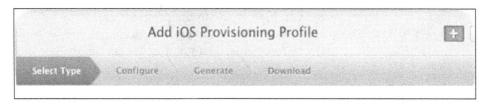

- **Select Type**: In the first screen, you can choose whether the profile you are going to generate is going to be the one for development that will be used to make the development/test build or the one for distribution that will be used to make the final store build. So, keep in mind what you will choose now; you will have to carry out the same steps again to generate the other one. At the end of the day, you will need to make both build types in the process of making any iOS game. So, ensure that you select **iOS App Development** in one instance and **App Store** in the other instance.

- **Select App ID**: On the second screen, you will need to select your App ID. So, if it is your first time creating a game/app, then you will find only one App ID that we already generated earlier in the second section of the iOS developer portal panel. However, if you have made several App IDs before, then you need to pick the correct one.

- **Select certificate**: In this screen, you will need to select the correct certificate. As you can see, this screen looks like a smart one. If you are already generating a Development Provisioning Profile, the screen will show you only the development certificates, from which you have to select the correct one (in case you have more than one), and if you are generating a Distribution Provisioning Profile, it will list only the distribution certificates. Pick the correct one and click on **Continue**.

- **Select devices**: This is not a mandatory screen. What I mean is that it is not necessary to see it every time you generate a profile. For example, if you are generating a development profile, you must see this screen, as it will ask you to select the authorized devices to run the game/app. However, if you are generating a Distribution Provisioning Profile, it does make sense to never ask you to select devices, as the game will be published and should be running on any valid device that downloaded/purchased it in the correct way via the App Store.

- **Name the profile**: Feel free to use any name that you can identify later. Usually, you enter the game name with a word, for example `Development` or `Developer`, that will make your organizer in XCode look a lot more clean and organized. Also, as this will be our last screen in the process, you will see that it shows the choices you have made in the previous steps and tells you the type, App ID, certificates, and the number of devices that will be listed in the profile. Ensure that you have entered a good name and all the choices are correct. Now, hit the **Generate** button.

- **Download**: The process of generating the profile will take a few seconds and then will automatically take you to a download screen; you can/must download this profile. Then, redo the same process for a profile of the other type (development or distribution). After you finish the process for the other file, keep those files in a safe place, as we will use them later. Keep in mind that with each new game we create, we will need to generate a new App ID and only two provisioning profiles (development and distribution). The certificate and devices will remain the same, except if you want to add new devices or change the certificate or update it in case it expires.

Now you've made one of the most important steps in your iOS game development pipeline. No matter what you will make inside the editor, without a valid provisioning profile, you will not be able to test in your device or publish the game to the App Store.

Summary

Now, you have completed the process of getting UE4 source code or a precompiled version and getting your own developer account. You have also learned how to build your own Unreal Engine version using the GitHub source code within XCode, and set the whole thing up correctly to avoid any errors/issues in the future.

Building a game profile is essential to start making and testing any iOS game using UE4 or any other technology. Now, you will not only be able to make a game profile, but also build a developer certificate from scratch and associate some devices as test devices.

Now, with all of this in your pocket, it is time to run Unreal Engine and start building the stepping stones for all the games we are going to make in this book. Making an iOS game requires some procedures inside Unreal Engine regardless of the game type, genre, or inputs. In *Chapter 2*, *Methods and Tools to Create Your Games*, we will prepare a sample project, which will be the core of many of our upcoming games. Also, we will discuss the techniques and methods that can be used to build our games. So, if you are ready, turn the page and jump directly to *Chapter 2*, *Methods and Tools to Create Your Games*. However, if you have not built a game profile yet, then ensure that you can build one first!

2
Methods and Tools to Create Your Games

When Unreal Engine 4 was made available to the public in early 2014, it held within its new features, a new major feature called the *Blueprints* editor. Everyone expected that the engine would still use and support the *Kismet* editor from Unreal Engine 3, but we found that Epic removed it and replaced it with a brand new and more powerful editor for game/gameplay logic scripting.

In the course of this book, we'll use this new system to build up our content and games, and in this chapter, we'll cover the following topics:

- Blueprints inside Unreal and its usage and types
- iOS platform-specific nodes
- Blueprints—tips and tricks
- iOS project pipeline with Unreal
- Setting up project settings
- Building into a device

Blueprints inside Unreal Engine

Essentially, a blueprint makes everything in the game logic clear and easy to follow. When creating a game with UE4, a blueprint does exactly this: makes writing code or game logic much easier.

If you have had the chance to work with the free, limited version of Unreal Engine 3, which was UDK, you will know that the scripting inside UDK was based on one of two things: either using the scripting language called *Unreal Script*, or using Kismet.

The Blueprints system in UE4 is almost the only, and certainly the most common way to build game logic efficiently and fast. It is the new version of the old system in UE3 called Kismet, that was not efficient when it came to refactoring the logic for different levels inside the same game. The engine supports C++ game code as well, but in that case I would not consider it as scripting, as C++ cannot be a scripting language and is pure programming!

With a simple graph of four nodes like the following one, you will be able to save the time taken to write code. The following graph says that:

- If the player presses **Jump**, then the character controller executes the respective jump function
- If the player inputs Horizontal axis, then the controller will use the Add Movement function with a specific amount of moment, and a direction (values passed through the function).

To write similar code in any programming language, you would spend 10 minutes and write at least 50 lines of code, but with a blueprint, all that you need is 4 nodes and 5 seconds of your time! For more efficient usage of the blueprints system, if you are a programmer, you can write your own blueprint node in C++ that executes a set of functionalities. This will save you the time taken to connect several nodes or write lots of code multiple times.

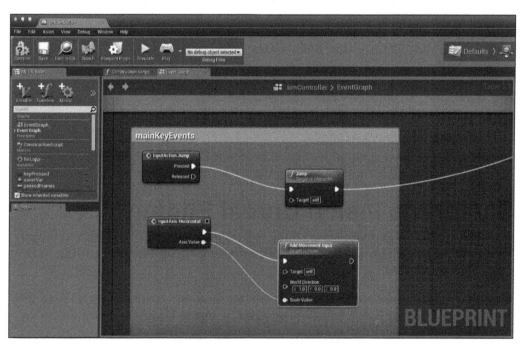

Different types of blueprints

There are two types of blueprints; when you start building logic for each of them, you will be using the same nodes with similar mechanisms. However, each type has its own usage and its own way to execute. The different types of blueprints are:

- **The class blueprint**: This is the most commonly used blueprint type during the process of building the gameplay elements. The easiest way to think about it is that each entity in the world is a blueprint as long as the entity has to act, behave, or do any logic type. These types of blueprints are very powerful, as you can use them anywhere inside your project; you can even recycle them to be used in another project somehow! You can have any number of these; it depends on your game and world size and complexity. A good example of a class blueprint can be an enemy blueprint or a collectable object.

- **The level blueprint**: As the previous type is a per-entity or per-object blueprint, this one is a per-level blueprint. This means that each level has its own blueprint that can be used only in the same level, and is used to control the current level entities and blueprints. Connecting some cloud objects with raindrop particles is a good example of what a level blueprint can achieve.

  As they are only exposed per-level, this means that their number will always be limited to your number of levels; so if your project contains 20 maps/levels, it means that you have *exactly* 20 level blueprints!

The need for blueprints

Choosing blueprints to make the course for this book came as a result of a hard decision. As a programmer, I like to write code all the time, even when working with node-based editors such as Unreal's blueprint system. I still tend to write pseudo code first to arrange my ideas and then apply this code to the engine in the shape of blueprint node connections. So, here are the major reasons that will make us use blueprints:

- As I mentioned earlier, blueprints are not a code-based system; a beginner can understand them and can start building stuff and improvising from the lessons here and building new content. A new programmer can understand the basics of programming and the construction of game/gameplay code from node-based graphs.

  A hardcore programmer can learn how to adapt his vast knowledge to the modern scripting editors.

  Game designers or perhaps artists can also use it to build gameplay logic, levels and construction scripts, or game systems and subsystems.

  In spite of being a programmer, it took me some time to adapt to the blueprints and node-based programming editors in general, as it is a process of generating code without writing it, which is totally different from what I have used over the years.

- Blueprints give you full access to all of the engine functions and methods. Using the blueprints doesn't mean that you will miss some parts of the engine; you will have full access to all you need in order to build the most complex game logic by controlling all of the game elements, such as audio, physics, rendering, animations, and inputs.

- With blueprints, you can make small logic changes and run it directly. All that you need to do is click on **Save**, and then you are free to hit the play button to test your logic. However, using code like C++ requires that you build or compile, which is a bit time consuming in the long run, especially if you are a person who likes to make sure that every piece runs fine and acts as it should before moving on to build a new part of the game logic.

- As blueprints are not a text-based method, it saves you some time , disk space, and money that would have otherwise been spent to purchase and install an IDE to use. If you are going to use blueprints only with Unreal, and you have no intention of making any changes with the engine source code, I would recommend that you directly download the prebuilt version. Keep in mind that you still need XCode on your computer to be able to make a real build on your device, otherwise you can keep testing in the editor safely.

- Some people have reported that blueprints are slow, maybe ten times slower than C++ Unreal Engine-based projects, but my advice for you is to ignore such heresy and to go and try it yourself! I used both systems and I could not find any difference: both games-based systems run fine for me on Windows, Mac, Android, iOS, and HTML5. It might be slower in the editor, but a final build ran equally in both, and any lag that came with a huge logic load was only due to the conversion the editor made at runtime to change the nodes into executable code.

What is a node?

A node is the visual representation of a function. To make life easier, Unreal Engine 4 provides the ability to create logic without writing code, by just using and connecting nodes.

A node can have inputs, outputs, both, or, in some cases, nothing except the execution ports.

For example, a **PrintString** node is a visual representation of the typical printing function, but has even more parameters. You can pass a string value to the **In String** input, or a Boolean value to the print options, or even a color variable to **TextColor**; however, as you can see, the nodes have no outputs. The white in and out arrows are not considered inputs or outputs, they are the function start and end, which represent the curly braces in a normal function.

Another example can be a node like **Event Hit**, which is an event node having no inputs, and usually has no execution as it executes itself. However, as you can see, it has lots of outputs, which always vary based on the current situation of the hit event.

The iOS/Mobile-only nodes

Unreal Engine is a cross-platform engine, which means that you write one block of code and then deploy it to several platforms, but not all nodes are made as general nodes to be used with all platforms. But there are a few nodes that are platform-specific, or in other words are nodes that can be run and executed successfully only on specific platforms:

- **Input Touch**: This is one of the functions/events that get executed automatically. Whenever the player touches his screen, this function will return the finger index and the touch coordinates. With this returned information, you can do all of the input magic that can be done for a touch screen device.

  You have two choices when the player touches: either execute the rest of the code when the touch starts, or when it is released.

- **Event Begin Input Touch**: This is an event by actor, which means it gets executed when the actor holding the node in its graph *gets touched* while click events are enabled.

- **Event End Input Touch**: This is an event by actor, which means it gets executed when the actor holding it in its graph gets *touch ended* while click events are enabled.

- **Event Touch Enter**: This is an event by actor, which means it gets executed when the actor holding it in its graph gets a *touch moved over* it while click events are enabled.

- **Event Touch Leave**: This is an event by actor, which means it gets executed when the actor holding it in its graph gets *a touch moved over it and left* while click events are enabled.

- **Write Leaderboard Integer**: This allows you to write a leaderboard integer value for a state name and submit it. It requires a player controller (which is the current class used by the player to control and navigate), a state name (which is a representation of the leaderboard value on the game center), and the value of this state. This returns just one value: either `true` or `false` indicating the successful or otherwise completion of the process.

- **Read Leaderboard Integer**: This queries for the value of an integer (`Stat Name`). This function requires two inputs: the stat name and the player controller. It can succeed and return the integer value to you as a **Leaderboard Value**, or it can fail for some reason, such as no connection to the Internet.

- **Flush Leaderboards**: As its name implies, this flushes the leaderboard values into the database. This requires the player controller as the input, as all other online services do, and the session name which is the same as **State Name** too.

- **Show Platform Specific Leaderboard Screen**: This gets executed when the player wants to check the leaderboard screen. It opens either the Google Play services leaderboard or the Game Center leaderboard depending on the running platform. It takes only a string value, which is the category name, as an input, and is the same as `State Name` from the read and write leaderboard functions.

- **Cache Achievements**: Executing this starts caching and fetching the player saved achievement's progress from the online service (Google Play or Game Center), and it can succeed or fail depending on the connection, as shown in the following screenshot:

- **Cache Achievements Description**: This works in a similar manner as **Cache Achievements**, except that it fetches the achievement's description itself. So it fetches the ID info to the device (such as the achievement name or proper text based on the achievement state), depending on whether he has unlocked this Achievement ID or it is still locked. Also, sometimes you have to change the description, let's say, to fix a typo, then it needs to be updated on the player's device.

- **Get Cached Achievements Progress**: With the achievement ID, you can start using the data you've already fetched via **Cache Achievements**, perhaps by sending it to the UI to show it on the screen. The node can return two values; the first one is a Boolean of either True or False with regard to the existence of the ID. The other returned value is the result itself as a float value named **Progress**.

- **Get Cached Achievements Description**: With the achievement ID, you can start using the data you've already fetched via **Cache Achievement Description**, perhaps by sending it to the UI to show it on the screen. The node can return several values, the first is a Boolean of either True or False with regard to the existence of the ID. **Get Cached Achievement Description** returns the achievement name/title, so you can use it as a title for the achievement in your UI or in your notification screen. It also returns the proper text to be used. In case the achievement is **Locked** or **Unlocked**, then you can display the correct ones based on the player's current state.

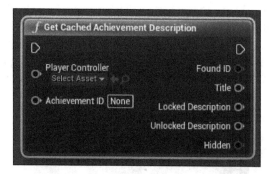

- **Write Achievement Progress**: Whenever the player unlocks an achievement locally, you will need to save it to the online system you are using. This node allows you to do this by adding a name/ID to the achievement to be used to fetch it in later sessions. You also need to input a value for it. The same inputs are returned after finishing to ensure that it was sent to its correct place with its correct value.

- **Show Platform Specific Achievements Screen**: If you want to have an **Achievements** button in your game that aims to open the Game Center achievements screen or Google Play achievement screen, using this node will allow you to pop up this screen directly.

- **EXPERIMENTAL Show Ad Banner**: If you are going to use ads in your game to earn money, then you will never find anything easier than Unreal Engine to handle it. By executing this node, you force the game to show ads, and as you can see, it has only one parameter as an input. By marking **Show on Bottom Of Screen**, the ad banner will be shown at the bottom, but if you set the check box to false, the banner will appear on the top of the screen. Keep in mind that it is named **EXPERIMENTAL** as it is not finalized yet. While you are reading this book, you might find the name is different; which may mean that it is officially released.

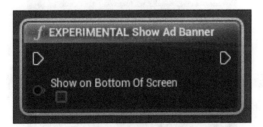

- **EXPERIMENTAL Hide Ad Banner**: This is also an experimental function aimed at hiding the banner, but still being able to show it again as it is still running, behind the player view. Note that it has no inputs or outputs, you just execute it.

- **EXPERIMENTAL Close Ad Banner**: This is another experimental node for ads. Using this node you can terminate/close the current banner, and then you can initialize a new banner using **Show Ad Banner**. This node has no inputs or outputs.

- **Get Input Motion State**: Using this function will return a set of useful coordinates to be used for device tilting, acceleration, and rotation-based games. It is normally known as an accelerometer or gyroscope in mobile devices.

 One important thing to note about this node is that it can only be found in a blueprint of the `PlayerController` class type. Also, it returns 4 different vector values: **Tilt**, **Rotation Rate**, **Gravity**, and **Acceleration**.

Blueprints – tips and tricks

The blueprints editor, like any other editor in the world, has its own hidden tricks that can be useful. This doesn't mean that you wouldn't be productive without it, but these tips and tricks make your life easier and help you progress faster. Since the engine was released, I started to sail in the blueprint editor world to figure out how I can make the best use of it. I found this:

- The thing that most of the users don't know is that the blueprint editor is not limited to using the mouse keys to navigate, manipulate, and connect nodes. There are many hot keys that can help you attain faster work flow. For a full list of the hot keys, you can refer to the documentation at `https://docs.unrealengine.com/latest/INT/Engine/Blueprints/UserGuide/CheatSheet/index.html`.

- Inserting nodes using right-click in the editor can be tricky. Right-clicking in an empty area will show you the nodes menu named **All Actions for this Blueprint** with all of the available nodes in the Unreal Engine editor for the current blueprint. This might be too complex for you sometimes, especially if you are a new developer.

   However, when you draw a line from an output node, you will find a small tooltip with the text **Place a new node**. If you release the mouse button in an empty area, the menu that appears named with the dragged node name (in my case **Flipbook**), contains *only* those nodes that can fit and work correctly with the output socket you used for this drag action.

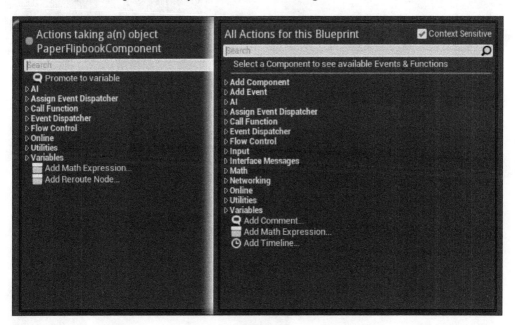

- When you use custom functions or events, if you double-click on the function/call, it will move your graph to show you the original function/ structure so that you can make changes to it. It is a very useful trick, which can save much of your time if your graphs are gigantic.

- When you add a new variable, let's say a Boolean (which means it is a variable that takes either a `True` or `False` value), you will be unable to set a variable's default value until you press the **Compile** button in the top-left corner of the editor. So, as with the code, you need to compile and run to see the result, but in a faster way. Then the question mark on the button will change to a true green mark post, after which the default values will be editable.

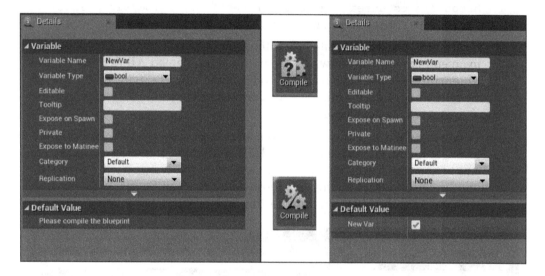

- After making a blueprint from any class type, let's say **Character Blueprint**, you will still be able to change the blueprint to a different class type. Sometimes, there will be some nodes that will be missed as not all of the blueprint classes share the same nodes, and sometimes you will get errors that need to be fixed; but at the end of the day, you can change a blueprint from a class type to another class type. All you have to do is click on the **Blueprint Props** button from the top shelf of your blueprint graph editor and this will activate a panel on your right-hand side.

In this new panel, you need to change **Parent Class** to any desired class. To be sure that the change has been made correctly, you will find that Character.h or whatever the first class name in the top-right corner of the graph editor will change to the new class name.

The iOS project pipeline

Through the next four chapters, we will be building four different games using Unreal Engine 4. There is no specific project pipeline that we should follow, but over the years, I have found that there are so many things that if organized early, will help us in our building and testing processes later. So here are the recommended and repetitive steps that you will need to perform for each game.

I prefer to explain these steps for setting up a project and getting it ready here, so that in each game chapter you can just go through the steps required to build the game and not the project and then the game. So, this part will be a reference for you, which you will need to execute at the beginning of each game, until you get used to that pipeline or invent your own way to prepare an iOS project with Unreal Engine.

Building the game's provisioning profiles

If you have been following the book from the first chapter, then you would know what a game profile is, and how and where to build it. So, first things first, you need to build two profiles for your game: development and distribution. Remember that both of them will be useless if you don't have installed certificates too.

Setting up the game provisioning profile

Epic gives you two choices regarding the setup of your game provisioning profiles. So you can put both files in either of these two places:

* Engine/Build/IOS/UE4Game.mobileprovision
* (Your Game Directory) /Build/IOS/(your Game Name). mobileprovision

In the first case, you can place your provisioning profiles directly in the engine directory, but in that case you must name the profile UE4Game. This is not a good idea if you are going to work with more than one game at the same time, as you must keep that naming.

The second method, which I prefer to use, is a per-project method. In this, you place both of your provisioning profiles in your game directory inside the `Build/ IOS` director. You must then name both of your files with the game name, and the distribution one should have the `Distro_` prefix.

For example, for the first game project that I'll be building in *Chapter 3*, *Creating a Brick Breaking Game*, the game profiles will be:

- **Development**: `Game / Build/IOS/bricksbreakingPacket. mobileprovision`
- **Distribution** : `BricksBreakingGame/ Build/IOS/ Distro_ bricksbreakingPacket. mobileprovision`

Creating a new project

Whenever you run Unreal Engine, the project window pops up giving you the choice to either run an old project or build a new one. There are four major things you should note in this window if you switch to the **New Project** tab:

- You can select a different directory to build your own projects rather than building them in the `Documents/Unreal Engine` directory. You just need to click on the small down arrow button next to the project name input field.

- There is an option called **Include starter content**, which should be unchecked, as this choice will add too many blueprints, models, and assets to your project. It is fine to add these if you are going to learn about them, or if you are going to build a game that has the look of those assets. However, during the process of our four games here, we will not need to use those assets, so let's save some space in our project by unchecking it.

- When you are going to give your project a name, ensure that you type the name without spaces and that it has less than 20 characters, otherwise you will get an error. For example, in the first game project, I named the project `BricksBreakingGame` rather than `Bricks Breaking Game`. The engine should give you feedback with a red error if you forget this.

- There are many start templates to use to build your game, some of them based on C++ code and the others based on blueprints. Normally, you should select a **Blank** template (which is the first one), otherwise I'll mention which template we are going to base our game on in the respective chapter.

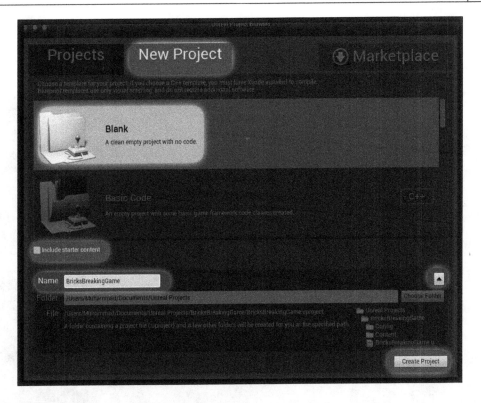

Editing the project settings

After naming your project and clicking on **Create Project**, the engine will take a while to set it up and load it. When the editor opens and completes loading, you can navigate to the **Edit** menu and select **Project Settings**.

There are some steps that need to be carried out here to make the project ready for iOS development. As you can see, you have different tabs in the left-hand side panel. You can add a project name and company info to your **Description** screen. You can set up the game levels and the default map in your **Maps** and **Modes** screen.

You can make so many changes to your project, but the four most important screens to which we want to make changes should be as follows:

- **Supported Platforms**: You need to ensure that iOS is supported for the project.

- **Input**: Ensure that you mark **Use Mouse for Touch** to enable the mouse clicks to be considered as touch input. Ensure that you disable **Always Show Touch Interface** and **Show Console on Four Finger Tap**, and clear **Default Touch Interface**. If there is a project which has different input configurations, it will be mentioned in the respective project chapter.

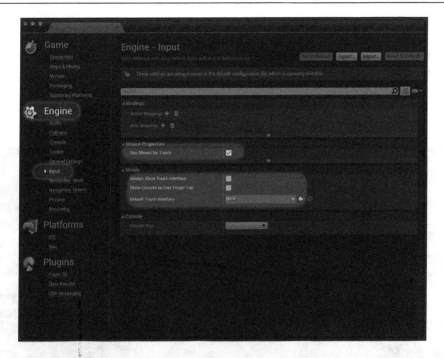

- **Rendering**: Switch off **Mobile HDR**, as none of our games will need it. All of our games will be 2D and are not based on light as they are based on shaders.

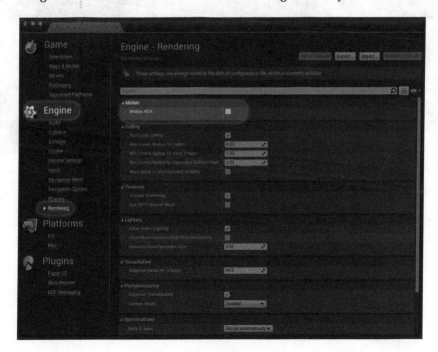

- **iOS**: If the game has online features, we will use **Enable Game Center Support**. However, I prefer to keep it switched off for now, as the online features will be discussed later in *Chapter 7, Monetizing your Game*. You will now see that all of the iOS options are grayed out and there is a warning message telling you that the project needs to be configured. So click on **Configure Now** and it will enable everything and make the project match our targeted platform.

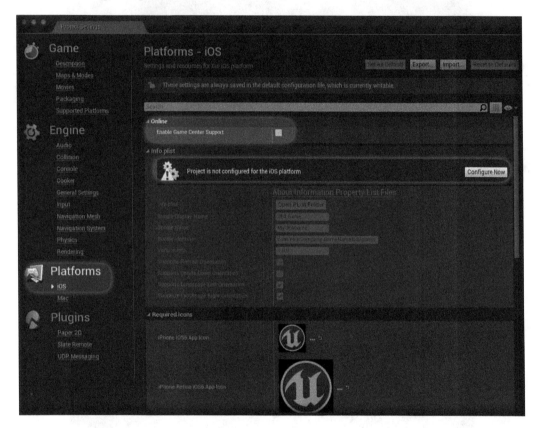

Editing the *.plist file

After configuring the project for iOS, you will have an `info.Plist` file generated for your project. You can either click on the **Open PList Folder** button or navigate to the `GameProject/Build/IOS` directory, and you will find a text file with your game's name and the `.plist` extension. Open this file and change the two string values `<key>CFBundleURLName</key>` and `<key>CFBundleIdentifier</key>` to the one you used while building the provisioning profile. In my case, it is `com.Muhammad.BriksBreakingForBook`. You should have something like this:

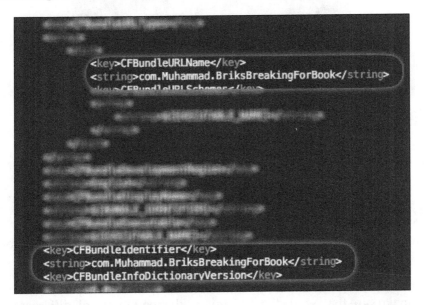

Feel free to dig more and investigate the PLIST file. It looks like a small and simple text file, but the fact is that this file can twist your iOS product by 180 degrees. For example, with some tweaks inside the PLIST file you can change the final game executable file name or add a glass effect to the game icon, change the game version number or even switch the game WiFi feature off. In a nutshell, this file is the director and manger that feeds the game/app with all of the information that should distinguish it.

Building a project

With earlier versions of Unreal, building a project for iOS wasn't particularly easy. However, with UE4, you can now build and run your project with just one click. You have two different options for how you can build your project into your device: launching and packaging.

Launching

Launching allows you to launch only the current level to test it in your device. It can be accessed from the top shelf of your editor, and when you press the little arrow button, it will give you a list of the available devices that you can launch the game into.

Packaging

Packaging allows you to build an *.ipa file, you can use any other application to push this file into your device to test it.

In addition to packaging the game, you need to navigate to **File | Package Project | IOS** and make sure that, while the packaging sub menu may look different for you, it will always contain the platforms supported by your OS. Currently, Mac supports only iOS and Mac, and Windows supports Windows, iOS, and Android.

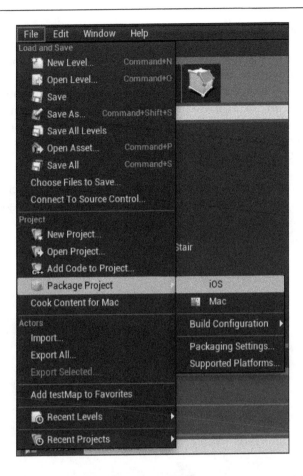

I always like to make a build for my empty project before I start adding content. This way, I can ensure that I set up the project correctly, rather than adding content and then getting a build failure, which will put me in a situation where I wouldn't know if the failure is a result of my incorrect content or incorrect project setup. So with each chapter, after preparing your game project, make an empty build to the device, just to ensure that you can push it correctly to the device.

Summary

Now, you are aware of a whole new concept of gameplay scripting, and the why and how of using it. You learned about the several types of blueprints, when to use each of them, how you can change a class blueprint type at any time you want, and how to keep it clean from errors. You are now also able to create a clean Unreal Engine 4 project from scratch and set it up correctly to match the iOS platform. Building and running a project with different build types is something essential for testing over time and now you know how easy it has become.

The next step for you is to start making games and learn how to script a gameplay. In the next chapter, we will begin a journey to build a physics-based game.

3
Creating a Brick Breaking Game

Have you ever thought about procedurally generated levels? Have you thought about how this could be done, how their logic works, and how their resources are managed?

With our example bricks game, you will get to the core point of generating colors procedurally for each block, every time the level gets loaded.

Physics has always been a huge and massively important topic in the process of developing a game. However, a brick breaking game can be made in many ways and using the many techniques that the engine can provide, but I choose to make it a physics-based game to cover the usage of the new, unique, and amazing component that Epic has recently added to its engine.

The `Projectile` component is a physics-based component for which you can tweak many attributes to get a huge variation of behaviors that you can use with any game genre.

By the end of this chapter, you will be able to:

- Build your first multicomponent blueprints
- Understand more about the game modes
- Script a touch input
- Understand the `Projectile` component in depth
- Build a simple emissive material
- Use the dynamic material instances
- Start using the construction scripts

- Detect collisions
- Start adding sound effects to the game
- Restart a level
- Have a fully functional gameplay

The project structure

If you are going to use the already finished project that comes with this book, then you will find that it was made with Unreal Editor 4.30. If you are using a higher version, it might tell you that the project will be upgraded to a higher version, which is not possible. Just keep this in mind!

For this game sample, I made a blank project template and selected to use the starter content so that I could get some cubes, spheres, and all other 3D basic meshes that will be used in the game. So, you will find the project structure still in the same basic structure, and the most important folder where you will find all the content is called **Blueprints**.

Building the blueprints

The game, as you might see in the project files, contains only four blueprints. As I said earlier, a blueprint can be an object in your world or even a piece of logic without any physical representation inside the game view. The four blueprints responsible for the game are explained here:

- `ball`: This is the blueprint that is responsible for the ball rendering and movement. You can consider it as an entity in the game world, as it has its own representation, which is a 3D ball.

- `platform`: This one also has its visual representation in the game world. This is the platform that will receive the player input.

- `levelLayout`: This one represents the level itself and its layout, walls, blocks, and game camera.

- `bricksBreakingMode`: Every game or level made with Unreal Engine should have a game mode blueprint type. This defines the main player, the controller used to control the gameplay, the pawn that works in the same way as the main player but has no input, the HUD for the main UI controller, and the game state that is useful in multiplayer games. Even if you are using the default setting, it will be better to make a space holder one!

Gameplay mechanics

I've always been a big fan of planning the code before writing or scripting it. So, I'll try to keep the same habit here as well; before making each game, I'll explain how the gameplay workflow should be. With such a habit, you can figure out the weak points of your logic, even if you didn't build it. It helps you develop quickly and more efficiently.

As I mentioned earlier, the game has only three working blueprints, and the fourth one is used to organize the level (which is not gameplay logic and has no logic at all). Here are the steps that the game should follow one by one:

1. At the start of the game, the `levelLayout` blueprint will start instantiating the bricks and set a different color for each one.

2. The `levelLayut` blueprint sets the rendering camera to the one we want.

3. The `ball` blueprint starts moving the ball with a proper velocity and sets a dynamic material for the ball mesh.

4. The `platform` blueprint starts accepting the input events on a frame-by-frame basis from mouse or touch inputs, and sets a dynamic material for the platform mesh.

5. If the `ball` blueprint hits any other object, it should never speed up or slow down; it should keep the same speed.

6. If the `ball` blueprint crossed the bottom line, it should restart the level.

7. If the player pressed the screen or clicked on the mouse, the `platform` blueprint should move only on the y axis to follow the finger or the mouse cursor.

8. If the `ball` blueprint hits any brick from the `levelLayout` blueprint, it should destroy it.

9. The ball plays some sound effects. Depending on the surface it hits, it plays a different sound.

Starting a new level

As the game will be based on one level only and the engine already gives us this new pretty level with a sky dome and light effects with some basic assets, all of this will not be necessary for our game. So, you need to go to the **File** menu, select **New Level**, add it somewhere inside your project files, and give it a special name. In my case, I made a new folder named `gameScene` to hold my level (or any other levels if my game is a multilevel game) and named it `mainLevel`.

Now, this level will never get loaded into the game without forcing the engine to do that. The Unreal Editor gives you a great set of options to define which is the default map/level to be loaded when the game starts or when the editor runs. Even when you ship the game, the Unreal Editor tells us which levels should be shipped and which levels shouldn't be shipped to save some space.

Open the **Edit** menu and then open **Project Settings**. When the window pops up, select the **Maps & Modes** section and set **Game Default Map** to the newly created level. **Editor Startup Map** should also have the same level:

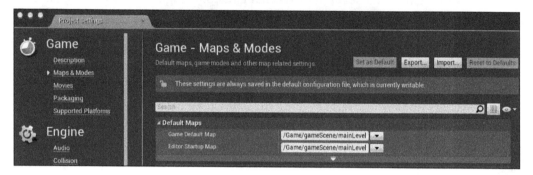

Building the game mode

Although a game mode is a blueprint, I prefer to always separate its creation from the creation of the game blueprints, as it contains zero work for logic or even graphs. A game mode is essential for each level, not only for each game.

Right-click in an empty space inside your project directory and select **Blueprint** under the **Basic assets** section. When the **Pick Parent Class** window pops up, select the last type of blueprint, which is called **Game Mode**, and give your newly created blueprint a name, which, in my case, is **bricksBreakingMode**.

Now, we have a game mode for the game level; this mode will not work at all without being connected to the current level (the empty level I made in the previous section) somehow.

Go to **World Settings** by clicking on the icon in the top shelf of the editor (you need to get used to accessing **World Settings**, as it has so many options that you will need to tweak them to fit your games):

The **World Settings** panel will be on the right-hand side of your screen. Scroll down to the **Game Mode** part and select the one you made from the **Game Mode Override** drop-down menu.

If you cannot find the one you've made, just type its name, and the smart menu will search over the project to find it.

Building the game's main material

As the game is an iOS game, we should work with caution when adding elements and code to save the game from any performance overhead, glitches, or crashes. Although the engine can run a game with the **Light** option on an iOS device, I always prefer to stay as far away as possible from using lights/directional lights in an iOS game, as a directional light source on mealtime would mean recalculating all the vertices. So, if the level has 10k vertices with two directional lights, it will be calculated as 30k vertices.

The best way to avoid using a light source for such a simple game like the brick breaking game is to build a special material that can emulate a light emission; this material is called an emissive material.

In your project panel, right-click in an empty space (perhaps inside the `materials` folder) and choose a material from the **Basic Assets** section. Give this material a name (which, in my case, is **gameEmissiveMaterial**) and then double-click to open the material editor.

As you can see, the material editor for a default new material is almost empty, apart from one big node that contains the material outputs with a black colored material. To start adding new nodes, you will need to right-click in an empty space of your editor grid and then either select a node or search for nodes by name; both ways work fine.

The emissive material is just a material with **Color** and **Emissive Color**; you can see these names in your output list, which means you will need to connect some sort of nodes or graphs to these two sockets of the material output.

Now, add the following three new nodes:

- `VectorParameter`: This represents the color; you can pick a color by clicking on the color area on the left-hand panel of the screen or on the **Default Value** parameter.

- `ScalarParameter`: This represents a factor to scale the color of the material; you can set its **Default Value** to **2**, which works fine for the game.

- `Multiply`: This will multiply two values (the color and the scalar) to give a value to be used for the emission.

With these three nodes in your graph, you might figure out how it works. The basic color has to be added to the base color output, and then the **Multiply** result of the base color and scalar will be added to the emissive color output of the material:

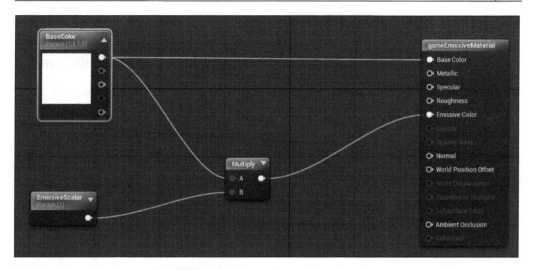

You can rename the nodes and give them special names, which will be useful later on. I named the **VectorParameter** node **BaseColor** and the **Scalar** node **EmissiveScalar**.

You can check out the difference between the emissive material you made and another default material by applying both to two meshes in a level without any light. The default material will light the mesh in black as it expects a light source, but the emissive one will make it colored and shiny.

Building the blueprints and components

I prefer to call all the blueprints for this game *actors* as all of them will be based on a class in the engine core. This class usually represents any object with or without logic in the level. Although blueprints based on the actor class are not accepting input, you will learn a way to force any actor blueprint to get input events. This is the reason for picking the actor class as a general class for the course of this book. In this section, you will build the different blueprints for the game and add components for each one of them. Later on, in another section, you will build the logic and graphs. As I always say, building and setting all the components and the default values should be the first thing you do in any game, and then adding the logic should follow. Do not work on both simultaneously!

Building the layout blueprint

The layout blueprint should include the bricks that the players are going to break, the camera that renders the level, and the walls that the ball is going to collide with.

Start making it by adding an **Actor** blueprint in your project directory. Name it levelLayout and double-click on it to open the blueprint editor.

The blueprint editor, by default, contains the following three subeditors inside it; you can navigate between them via the buttons in the top-right corner:

- **Defaults**: This is used to set the default values of the blueprint class type
- **Components**: This is used to add different components to build and structure the blueprint
- **Graph**: This is where we will add scripting logic

The majority of the time, you will be working with the components and graph editors only, as the default editor's default values always work the best:

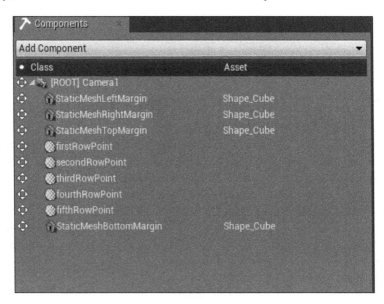

Open the component graph and start adding these components:

- **Camera**: This will be the component that renders the game. As you can see in the preceding screenshot, I added one component and left its name as **Camera1**. It was set as **ROOT** of the blueprint; it holds all the other components as children underneath its hierarchy.

  ○ **Changed Values**: The only value you need to change in the camera component is **Projection Mode**. You need to set it to **Orthographic**, as it will be rendered as a 2D game, and keep **Ortho Width** as **512**, as it will make the screen show all the content in a good size. Feel free to use different values based on the content of your level design.

>
> Orthographic cameras work without depth, and they are recommended more in 2D games. On the other hand, the perspective camera has more depth, and it is better to be used with any games with 3D content.

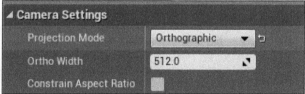

- **Static Mesh**: To be able to add meshes as boundaries or triggering areas to collide with the ball, you will need to add cubes to work as collision walls, perhaps hidden walls. The best way to add this is by adding four static meshes and aligning and moving them to build them as a scene stage. Renaming all of them is also a good way to go. To be able to distinguish between them, you can name them as I named them: **StaticMeshLeftMargin, StaticMeshRightMargin, StaticMeshTopMargin,** and **StaticMeshBottomMargin**. The first three are the left, right, and top margins; they will be working as collision walls to force the ball to bounce in different directions. However, the bottom one will work as a trigger area to restart the level when the ball passes through it.

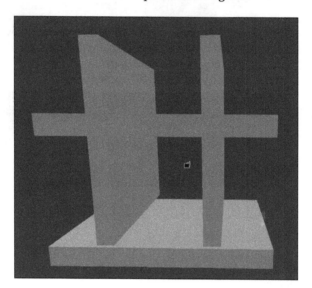

  - **Changed Values**: You need to set **Static Mesh** for them as the cube and then start to scale and move it to build the scene.

- For the walls, you need to add the **Wall** tag for the first three meshes in the **Component Tags** options area, and for the bottom trigger, you need to add another tag; something like **deathTrigger** works fine. These tags will be used by the gameplay logic to detect whether the ball hits a wall and you need to play a sound or whether it hits a death area and you need to restart the level.

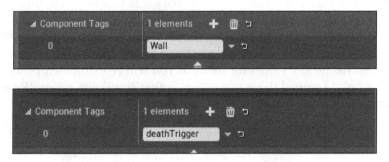

- In the **Collision** section for each static mesh, you need to set both **Simulation Generates Hit Events** and **Generate Overlap Events** to **True**. Also, for **Collision Preset**, you can select **Block All**, as this will create solid walls to block any other object from passing:

- Finally, from the **Rendering** options section, you need to select the emissive material we have made to be able to see those static meshes, and you need to mark **Hidden in Game** as **True** to hide those objects. Keep in mind that you can keep those objects in the game for debugging reasons, and when you are sure that they are in the correct place, you can move to this option again and remark it as **True**.

- **Billboard**: For now, you can think about the billboard component as a point in space with a representation icon, and this is how it is mostly used inside UE4 as the engine does not support an independent transform component yet. However, billboards have always been used to show the contents that always face the camera, such as particles, text, or any other thing you need to always get rendered from the same angle. As the game will be generating the blocks/bricks during the gameplay, you will need to have some points to define where to build or to start building those bricks. You can add five billboard points, rename them, and rearrange them to look like a column. You don't have to change any values for them, as you will be using their position in space values only! I named those five points as **firstRowPoint**, **SecondRowPoint**, **thirdRowPoint**, **fourthRowPoint**, and **fifthRowPoint**.

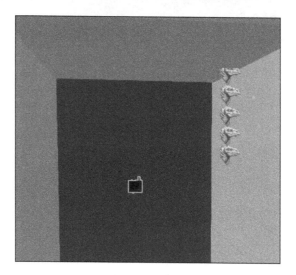

Building the ball blueprint

Start making the ball blueprint by adding an **Actor** blueprint in your project directory. Name it **Ball** and double-click on it to open the blueprint editor. Then, navigate to the **Components** subeditor if you are not ready. Start adding the following components to the blueprint:

- The sphere will work as the collision surface for the **Ball** blueprint. So, for this reason, you will need to set its **Collision** option to **Simulation Generates Hit Events** and **Generate Overlap Events** to **True**. Also, set the **Collision Preset** option to **Block All** to act in a manner similar to the walls from the layout blueprint. You need to set the **Sphere Radius** option from the **Shape** section to **26.0** so that it is of a good size that fits the screen's overall size.

- The process for adding static meshes is the same as you did earlier, but this time, you will need to select a sphere mesh from the standard assets that came with the project. You will also need to set its material to the project default material you made earlier in this chapter. Also, after selecting it, you might need to adjust its **Scale** to **0.5** in all three axes to fit the collision sphere size. Feel free to move the static mesh component on the x, y, and z axes till it fits the collision surface.

- The projectile movement component is the most important one for the **Ball** blueprint, or perhaps it is the most important one throughout this chapter, as it is the one responsible for the ball movement and velocity and for its physics behaviors. After adding the components, you will need to make some tweaks to it to allow it to give the behavior that matches the game. Keep in mind that any small amount of change in values or variables will lead you to have a completely different behavior, so feel free to play through the values and test them to get some crazy ideas about what you can achieve and what you can get.

- For changed values, you need to set **Projectile Gravity Scale** to **0.0** from within the **Projectile** options; this will allow the ball to fly in the air without a gravity force to bring it down (or any other direction for a custom gravity).

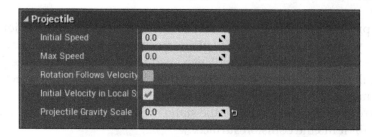

- For **Projectile Bounces**, you will need to mark **Should Bounce** as **True**. In this case, the projectile physics will be forced to keep bouncing with the amount of bounciness you set. As you want the ball to keep bouncing over the walls, you need to set the value to **1.0** to give it full bounciness power:

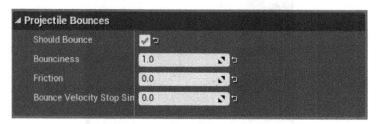

- From the **Velocity** section, you will need to enter a velocity for the ball to start using when the game runs; otherwise, the ball will never move. As you want the first bounce of the ball to be towards the blocks, you need to set the **Z** value to a high number, such as **300**, and give it more level design sense. It shouldn't bounce in a vertical line, so it is better to give some force on the horizontal axis **Y** as well as move the ball in a diagonal direction. So, let's add **300** into **Y** as well.

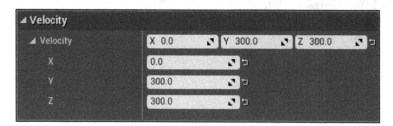

Building the platform blueprint

Start making the **platform** blueprint by adding an **Actor** blueprint in your project directory. Name it **platform** and double-click on it to open the blueprint editor. Then, navigate to the **Components** subeditor if you are not there already. You will add only one component, and it will work for everything. You want to add a **Static Mesh** component, but this time, you will be selecting the **Pipe** mesh; you can select whatever you want, but the pipe works the best.

Don't forget to set its material to be the same emissive material as we used earlier to be able to see it in the game view, and set its **Collision** option to **Simulation Generates Hit Events** and **Generate Overlap Events** to **True**. Also, **Collision Preset** should be set to **Block All** to act in the same manner as the walls from the layout blueprint.

Building the graphs and logic

Now, as all the blueprints have been set up with their components, it's time to start adding the gameplay logic/scripting. However, to be able to see the result of what you are going to build, you first need to drag and drop the three blueprints inside your scene and organize them to look like an actual level.

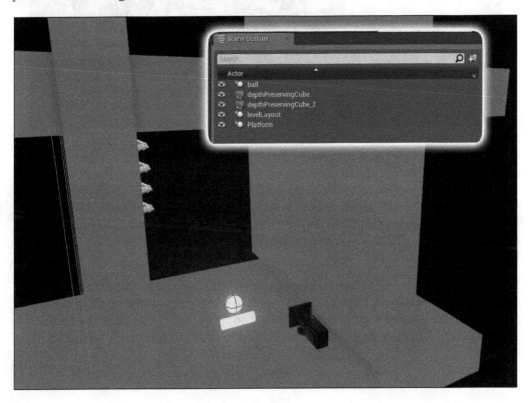

As the engine is a 3D engine and there is no support yet for 2D physics, you might notice that I added two extra objects to the scene (giant cubes), which I named **depthPreservingCube** and **depthPreservingCube2**. These objects are here basically to prevent the ball from moving in the depth axis, which is **X** in Unreal Editor. This is how both the new preserving cubes look from a top view:

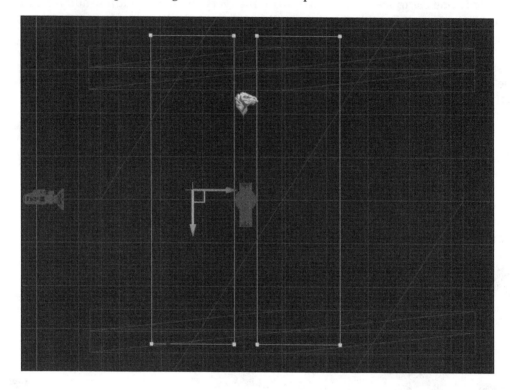

One general step that you will perform for all blueprints is to set the dynamic material for them. As you know, you made only one material and applied it to the platform and to the ball. However, you also want both to look different during the gameplay. Changing the material color right now will change both objects' visibility. However, changing it during the gameplay via the construction script and the dynamic material instances feature will allow you to have many colors for many different objects, but they will still share the same material.

So, in this step, you will make the platform blueprint and the ball blueprint. I'll explain how to make it for the ball, and you will perform the same steps to make it for the platform. Select the ball blueprint first and double-click to open the editor; then, this time navigate to the subeditor graphs to start working with the nodes.

You will see that there are two major tabs inside the graph; one of them is named **Construction Script**. This unique tab is responsible for the construction of the blueprint itself. Open the **Construction Script** tab that always has a **Construction Script** node by default; then, drag and drop the **StaticMesh** component of the ball from the panel on the left-hand side. This will cause you to have a small context menu that has only two options: **Get** and **Set**. Select **Get**, and this will add a reference to the static mesh.

Now, drag a line from **Construction Script**, leave it in an empty space, add a **Create Dynamic Material Instance** node from the context menu, and set its **Source Material** option to the material we want to instance (which is the emissive material). However, keep in mind that if you are using a later version, Epic introduces a more easy way to access the **Create Dynamic Material Instance** node by just dragging a line from **Static Mesh-ball** inside **Graph**, and not **Construction Script**.

Now, connect the static mesh to be the target and drag a line out of **Return Value** of the **Create Dynamic Material Instance** node. From the context menu, select the first option, which is **Promote to a Variable**; this will add a variable to the left-panel list. Feel free to give it a name you can recognize, which, in my case, is **thisColor**. Now, the whole thing should look like this:

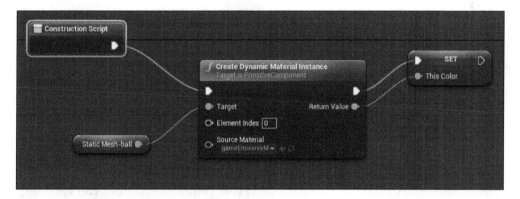

Now that you've created the dynamic material instance, you need to set the new color for it. To do this, you need to go back to the event graph and start adding the logic for it. I'll add it to the ball also, and you need to apply it again in **Event Graph** of the **platform** blueprint.

Add an **Event Begin Play** node, which is responsible for the execution of some procedurals when the game starts. Drag a wire out of it and select the **Set Vector Parameter Value** node that is responsible for setting the value for the material.

Now, add a reference for the **thisColor** variable and connect it to **Target** of the **Set Vector Parameter Value** node. Last but not least, enter **Parameter name** that you used to build the material, which, in my case, is **BaseColor**.

Finally, set **Value** to a color you like; I picked yellow for the ball. Which color would you like to pick?

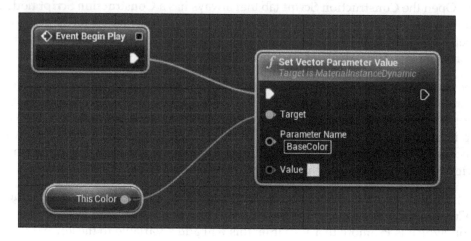

The layout blueprint graph

Before you start working with this section, you need to make several copies of the material we made earlier and give each one its own color. I made six different ones to give a variation of six colors to the blocks.

The scripts here will be responsible for creating the blocks, changing their colors, and finally, setting the game view to the current camera. To serve this goal, you need to add several variables with several types. Here are some variables:

- **numberOfColumns**: This is an integer variable that has a default value of six, which is the total number of columns per row.

- **currentProgressBlockPosition**: This is a vector type variable to hold the position of the last created block. It is very important because you are going to add blocks one after the other, so you want to define the position of the last block and then add spacing to it.

- **aBlockMaterial**: This is the material that will be applied to a specific block.

- **materialRandomIndex**: This is a random integer value to be used for procedural selected colors for each block.

To make things more organized, I managed to make several custom events. You can think about them as a set of functions; each one has a block of procedurals to execute:

- **Initialize The Blocks**: This **Custom Event** node has a set of `for` loops that are working one by one on initializing the target blocks when the game starts. Each loop cycles six times from **Index 0** to the number of columns index. When it is finished, it runs the next loop. Each loop body is a custom function itself, and they all run the same set of procedurals, except that they use a different row.

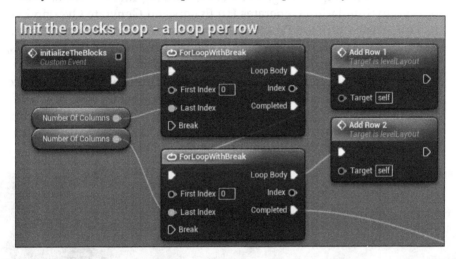

- **chooseRandomMaterial**: This custom event handles the process of picking a random material to be applied to in the process of creation. It works by setting a random value between 1 and 6 to the **materialRandomIndex** variable, and depending on the selected value, the **aBlockMaterial** variable will be set to a different material. This **aBlockMaterial** variable is the one that will be used to set the material of each created block in each iteration of the loop for each row.

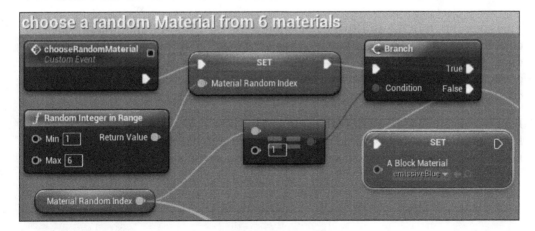

- **addRowX:** I named this **X** here, but in fact, there are five functions to add the rows; they are **addRow1**, **addRow2**, **addRow3**, **addRow4**, and **addRow5**. All of them are responsible for adding rows; the main difference is the start point of adding the row; each one of them uses a different billboard transform, starting from **firstRowPoint** and ending with **fifthRowPoint**. You need to connect your first node as **Add Static Mesh** and set its properties as any other static mesh. You need to set its material to the emissive one. Set **Static Mesh** to **Shape_Pipe_180**, give it a **brickPiece** tag, and set its **Collision** options to **Simulation Generates Hit Events** and **Generate Overlap Events** to **True**. Also, **Collision Preset** has to be set to **Block All** to act in the same manner as the walls from the layout blueprint and receive the hit events, which will be the core of the ball detection. This created mesh will need a transform point to be instantiated in its cords. This is where you will need to pick the row point transform reference (depending on your row, you will select the point number), add it to a **Make Transform** node, and finally, set the new transform **Y Rotation** to **-90** and its **XYZ scale** to **0.7, 0.7, 0.5** to fit the correct size and flip the block to have a better convex look.

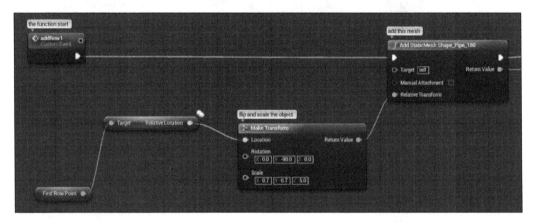

This second part of the **addRow** event should use the **ChooseRandomMaterial** custom event that you already made to select a material from among six random ones. Then, you can execute **SetMaterial**, make its **Target** the same mesh that was created via **Add Static Mesh**, and set its **Material** to **aBlockMaterial**; the material changes every time the **chooseRandomMaterial** event gets called.

Finally, you can use **SetRelativeLocation** of the billboard point that is responsible for that row to another position on the *y* axis, using the **Make Vector** and **Add Int(+)** nodes to add **75** units every time as a spacing between every two created blocks:

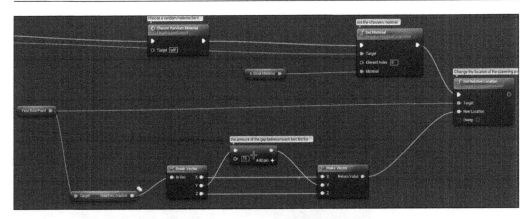

Now, if you check the project files, you will find that the only difference is that there are five functions called **addRow**, and each of them uses a different billboard as a starting point to add the blocks. Now, if you run the version you made or the one within the project files, you will be able to see the generated blocks, and each time you stop and run the game, you will get a completely different color variation of the blocks.

There is one last thing to completely finish this blueprint. As you might have noticed, this blueprint contains the camera in its components. This means it should be the one that holds the functionality of setting this camera to be the rendering camera. So, in **Even Begin Play**, this functionality will be fired when the level starts. You need to connect the **the Set View Target With Blend** node that will set the camera to the **Target** camera, and you need to connect **Get Player Controller** (player 0 is the player number 1) to the **Target** socket. This blueprint refers to **New View Target**. Finally, you need to call the **initializeTheBlocks** custom event, which will call all the other functions.

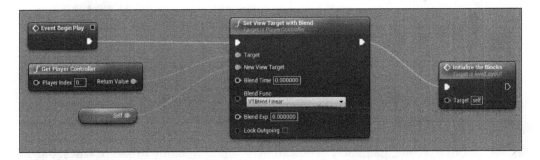

Congratulations! Now you have built your first functional and complex blueprint that contains the main and important functionalities everyone must use in any game. Also, you got the trick of how you can randomly generate or change things such as the color of the blocks to make the levels feel different every time.

The Ball blueprint graph

The main event node that will be used in the ball graph is **Event Hit**, which will be fired automatically every time the ball collider hits another collider. If you still remember, while creating the platform, walls, and blocks, we used to add tags for every static mesh to define them. Those names are used now. Using a node called **Component Has Tag**, we can compare the object component that the ball has hit with the value of the **Component Has Tag** node, and then, we either get a positive or negative result. So, this is how it should work:

- Whenever the ball gets hit with another collider, check whether it is a **brickPiece** tagged component. If this is true, then disable the collision of the brick piece via the **Set Collision Enabled** node and set it to **No Collision** to stop responding to any other collisions. Then, hide the brick mesh using the **Set Visibility** node and keep the **New Visibility** option unmarked, which means that it will be hidden. Then, play a sound effect of the hit to make it a more dynamic gameplay. You can play sound in many different ways, but let's use the **Play Sound at Location** node now, use the location of the ball itself, and use the **hitBrick** sound effect from the **Audio** folder by assigning it to the **Sound** slot of the **Play Sound at Location** node. Finally, reset the velocity of the ball using the **Set Velocity** node referenced by the **Projectile Movement** component and set it to **XYZ 300, 0, 300**:

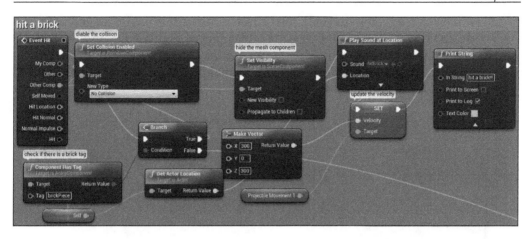

- If it wasn't a **brickPiece** tag, then let's check whether it is **Component Has Tag** of **Wall**. If this is the case, then let's use **Play Sound at Location**, use the location of the ball itself, and use the **hitBlockingWall** sound effect from the **Audio** folder by assigning it to the **Sound** slot of the **Play Sound at Location** node:

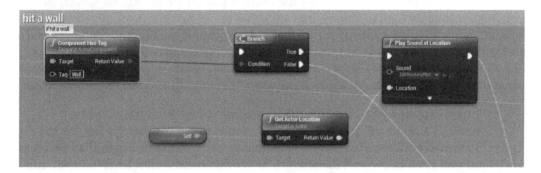

- If it wasn't tagged with **Wall**, then check whether it is finally tagged with **deathTrigger**. If this is the case, then the player has missed it, and the ball is not below the platform. So, you can use the **Open Level** node to load the level again and assign the level name as **mainLevel** (or any other level you want to load) to the **Level Name** slot:

The platform blueprint graph

The **platform** blueprint will be the one that receives the input from the player. As you learned in *Chapter 2, Methods and Tools to Create Your Games*, it is better to set **Use Mouse For Touch** in **Project settings** so you can write one logic and it works for both mouse input in the editor and for the touch input on the device. However, as you might remember, all the blueprints are based on an **Actor.h** class; this means, by default, they will not accept any input, and any scripting-based input will be ignored and will not give any result. So, you just need to define the player input to make the blueprint able to receive those events from the mouse, touch, or any other available input device. To do this, there are two ways, and I always like to use both these ways:

- **Enable input node**: I assume that you've already added the scripting nodes inside **Event graph** to set the dynamic material color via **Set Vector Parameter Value**. This means you already have an **Event Begin Play** node, so you need to connect its network to another node called **Enable Input**; this node is responsible for forcing the current blueprint to accept input events. Finally, you can set its **Player Controller** value to a **Get Player Controller** node and leave **Player Index** as **0** for the player number 1:

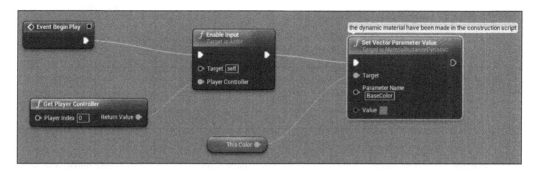

- **Autoreceive input option**: By selecting the **platform** blueprint instance that you've dropped inside the scene from the **Scene Outliner**, you will see that it has many options in the **Details** panel on the right-hand side. By changing the **Auto Receive Input** option to **Player 0** under the **Input** option, this will have the same effect as the previous solution:

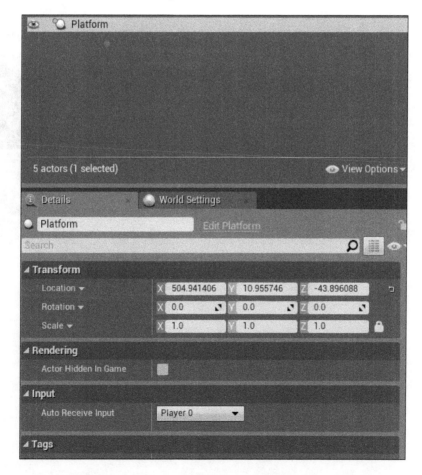

Now, we can build the logic for the platform movement, and anything that is built can be tested directly in the editor or on the device. I prefer to break the logic into two pieces, and this will make it easier than it looks like for you:

- **Get the touch state**: In this phase, you will use the **Input Touch** event that can be executed when a touch gets pressed or released. So based on the touch state, you will check via a **Branch** node whether the state is **True** or **False**. Your condition for this node should be **Touch 1 index**, as the game will not need more than one touch. Based on the state, I would like to set a custom Boolean variable named **Touched** and set its value to match the touch state. Then, you can add a **Gate** node to control the execution of the following procedurals based on the touch state (**Pressed** or **Released**) by connecting the two cases with the **Open** gate and the **Close** gate execution sockets. Finally, you can set the actor location and set it to use the **Self** actor as its target (which is the platform actor/blueprint) to change the platform location based on touches. Defining the **New Location** value is the next chunk of the logic:

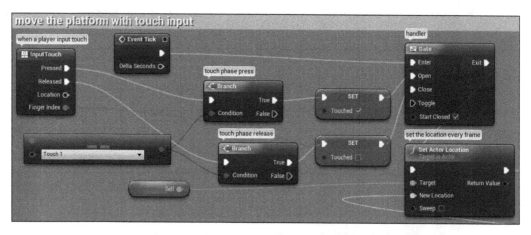

- **Actor location**: Using a **Make Vector** node, you can construct a new point position in the world made of X, Y, and Z coordinates. As the y axis will be the horizontal position, which will be based on the player's touch, only this needs to be changed over time. However, the X and Z positions will stay the same all the time, as the platform will never move vertically or in depth. The new vector position will be based on the touch phase. If the player is pressing, then the position should be matching the touch input position. However, if the players are not pressing, then the position should be the same as the last point the player had pressed. I managed to make a float variable named **horizontalAxis**; this variable will hold the correct Y position to be added to the **Make Vector** node. If the player is pressing the screen, then you need to get the finger press position by returning **Impact Point** by **Break Hit Result** via a **Get Hit Result Under Finger By Channel** node from the current active player. However, if the player is not touching the screen, then the **horizontalAxis** variable should stay the same as the last-know location for the **Self** actor. Then, it will set as it is into the **Make Vector** Y position value:

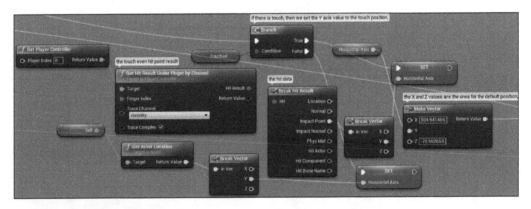

Now, you can save and build all the blueprints. Don't hesitate now or any time during the process of building the game logic to build or launch the game into a real device to check where you are.

The best way to learn more about the nodes and those minor changes is by building all the time into the divide and changing some values every time.

Summary

In this chapter, you went through the process of building your first Unreal iOS game. Also, you got used to making blueprints by adding nodes in different ways, connecting nodes, and adding several component types into the blueprint and changing its values.

Also, you learned how to enable input in an actor blueprint and get the touch and mouse input and fit them to your custom use.

You also got your hands on one of the most famous and powerful rendering techniques in the editor, which is called dynamic material instancing. You learned how to make a custom material and change its parameters whenever you want.

Procedurally, changing the look of the level is something interesting nowadays, and we barely scratched its surface by setting different materials every time we load the level. Later on, in *Chapter 5*, *Building an Exciting Endless Runner Game*, you will dive deeper into the procedural generation approach.

4

Advanced Game Content Generation with a Fruit Chopper Game

As I've mentioned before, physics has always been a huge and massively important topic in the process of developing a game, and we will keep using it with the majority of the games in this book, as there is no modern game that does not run on a physics system.

This is a book about iOS, yes? So, why not discuss the touch inputs, and how to recognize a swipe effect a bit more? Unreal Engine does not support the swipe action (at this moment, Version 4.3) by default, but there are many ways we can recognize it.

What makes players compete nowadays? Score! Let's scratch the surface and see how we can add scores to our games and wire the game to show it using UI text.

By the end of this chapter, you will be able to:

- Detect a swipe over a fruit
- Spawn actors during runtime
- Randomly generate objects
- Use different spawn points to give random gameplay
- Load a win or lose screen
- Add a UI text element
- Calculate the score
- Communicate different blueprints

- Build a particle system
- Get your hands on the Cascade editor
- Spawn particle emitters when needed
- Build a custom for loop using macros

The project structure

If you are going to browse the included project files, then you will find that they were made with Unreal Editor 4.30; if you are using a higher version, it might let you know that the project will be upgraded to a higher version, which is an irreversible step unless you are running your project within a version control system such as Git. Just keep that in mind!

For this game sample, I made a blank project template without the starter content. I got some photos of real fruit and sliced each picture into two pieces. For example, a banana will have three sprites, the full fruit and another two sprites of it splatted. The game is a 2D game, but following the same approach with 3D assets will let you get the same result. As for the folder structure, you will find the following contents:

- **The blueprints folder**: This contains all of the blueprints (regardless of types)
- **The levels folder**: This holds three levels, which are the game itself and another two small levels for the win and lose states
- **The materials folder**: This contains only one material that will be used for the particle system
- **The particles folder**: This contains one sample of the particle system that will be used as an effect for the chopping
- **The sprites folder**: This is the home for all of the textures and sprites you will need.

Importing the assets

In case you decided to start working from scratch with the provided assets (or maybe with your own unique assets), you will find a folder called fruitsResources with two other subfolders containing this chapter's files. The most important folder is the png folder, which contains all of the images after cutting them into pieces in Photoshop. Feel free to check the *.psd file or the sourceImages folder for the sources I found using Google.

Select all of the images inside the png folder and then drag-and-drop them inside the **Content Browser** window of your Unreal editor.

The images will look very strange and will not appear to have any sort of transparency, but they do in fact!

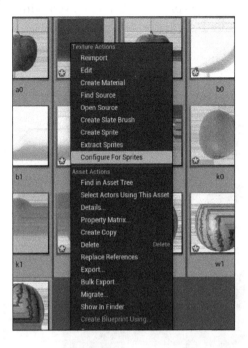

Select all of the images inside **Content Browser** and then right-click and select **Configure For Sprites** (or **Configure for Retro Sprites** for a later version of the editor). With this choice, **Content Browser** will start treating the imported texture assets. These assets will be used to build and construct sprites, and after this step, you will see them correctly with some transparency.

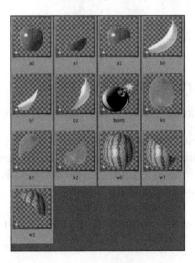

Select all of them again (if they are not already selected) and right-click on them again, but this time, pick **Create Sprite**. This will create a copy of each asset, but make sure the new ones are 2D sprites that can be used with Paper2D (the 2D system inside Unreal Engine).

Note that the ones framed in red are normal texture assets, but the ones framed in blue/cyan with a white background are sprites.

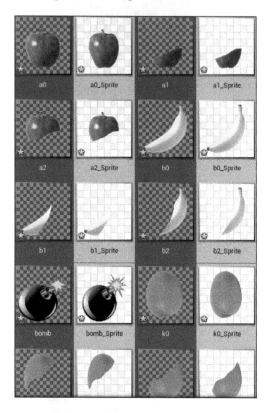

An overview of blueprints

Before you start, you must keep in mind that most of the blueprints run the same logic.

- **Apple, banana, kiwi, and watermelon**: All of the fruits are the same; in fact, I made the banana blueprint first and then duplicated it several times, changed the sprites to use different fruit textures, and finally, renamed them. So you can follow the same approach for a faster creation process. A fruit blueprint contains the logic to get touched by the player, chop the fruit into two pieces, show some particles, and finally, send a call to add the score.

- **bomb**: The player must have something to make the gameplay harder. Something to kill him/her. The bomb has almost the same construction and logic as the fruits, except for one part. When it is touched, it shows the player a lose screen rather than processing a chop and a score addition.

- **fruitsGame**: Here rests all of the logic for the gameplay. Inside this blueprint is all of the logic to instantiate the fruits and bombs in a random way in random positions. Also, it contains the UI for the score and the calculations to add scores or show the player a win or lose state.

- **winScreen**: This is a small blueprint having a camera and the text telling the player that he/she won. It runs in its own level file.

- **loseScreen**: This is the same as the **winScreen** blueprint, but it runs in a different level file and shows a different text message to the player.

- **fruitChopperMode**: This is a game mode, which is necessary for any Unreal game/level as discussed earlier in *Chapter 3, Creating a Brick Breaking Game*.

- **fruitChopperPlayerController**: This is a placeholder player controller to be used with the **fruitChopperMode** game mode blueprint class type. This can also be used to enable some mouse and touch events.

The gameplay mechanic

As mentioned in the previous game, which explains the mechanism of the gameplay loop, it will be better for you to work from scratch to understand the logic you got with the book. With that said, let's break down the gameplay logic:

1. Once the game starts, the **fruitsGame** blueprint will reset the score to zero and update its UI text. It will then start picking a random value for the fruits and the positions to be instantiated. It will then start shooting the fruits/bombs to the player.

2. The **fruitsGame** blueprint sets the rendering camera to the one we want.

3. The process of shooting fruits was set to shoot 70 fruits in all per level. You can change this, of course, but it is better to keep it in such a rage to kill the boredom of the long levels and gameplay sessions.

4. The shooting process contains a custom `for` loop, which you will learn to create. For this loop, you have to wait 0.7 seconds each time a loop is completed. After that, a random fruit blueprint is picked and a random point to shoot the next fruit/bomb is selected.

5. Each fruit will be moved by the physics component, and whenever the player touches it, it will add two sprites (chopped pieces) and destroy the full fruit sprite. It will then spawn the particles in the fruit's current position, and finally, search for **fruitsGame** and call its **AddScore** function to add the new score to the UI. However, if the player hits a **bomb** blueprint, it will call the **OpenLevel** function and open the **lose** level.

6. During **Event Tick** of **fruitsGame**, it will be looking forward to see if the player hit 50 in the **playerScore** variable; if yes, the game will show the **win** level.

The game levels

With the same method you already know, you will be creating 3 levels in this chapter. So, via the **File** menu and the **New Level** option, you will add three new levels. The first one for the gameplay itself, which I named **base** in my case, and the other two levels which will hold the game end screens. One of them I named **lose** and the other one, **win**. These two will be displayed based on the player's progression. Keep all of them empty at the moment until you figure out the blueprints you are going to use.

Building the particles

To make everything ready foe the game logic, I prefer building a quick particle system sample that will be displayed whenever the player correctly touches a fruit object. Building a particle system involves different steps starting with building a material for the particles, building the particles themselves and finally, spawning the particles. Let's start with the two main steps first and leave the spawning step until we reach part in the gameplay logic.

Building the material

Add a new material to **Content Browser** and name it **particlesMaterial**, then double click to open the material editor. Select its base node and set **Blend Mode** to **Translucent** and **Shading Model** to **Unlit**. With these two options, you will find some of the inputs the material has disabled as we will not need them with a typical particle material.

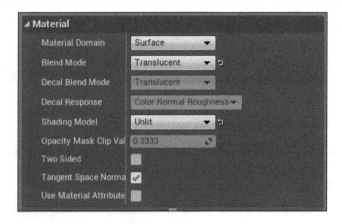

Now you can add the **RadialGradientExponential** node to your material grid, which will be responsible for showing a radial gradient shape (small particle shape) in the shaded surface.

Also, add a **Particle Color** node, which will hold the color of the particles (you will be able to change it later per instance). Now as you need to connect **color** to the material **Emissive Color** and **alpha** to the **Opacity** material input, you will need to add a **Multiply** node to multiply the **RadialGradientExponential** value to the **Particle Color** node values and display a correctly shaded particle at the end.

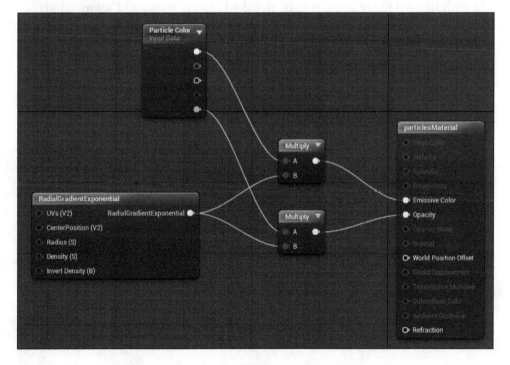

Building the particle system

To add a new particle system in the editor, you can just right-click inside your **Content Browser** and press **Particle System**. And it will add one directly! Name it (in my case, it is called **choppingParticles**) and then double-click on it to open the particle system editor (Cascade).

The Cascade editor is divided into four parts:

1. **Emitters**: This area holds your emitters. The powerful thing inside Unreal particles is that a particle system can have as many emitters as you want with different shapes and attributes.

2. It starts with one emitter which will be enough to make a sample for this game.

3. **Viewport**: This is a real-time view of your particle system, so you can check your progress as you go. You don't have to run in a game mode to check it!

4. **Details**: This is a dynamic sensitive area, where its content will change according to your current selected node, emitter, or option.

5. **Curve Editor**: Sometimes, entering the values will be better using curves rather than float numbers.

Emitter should be one entity, but in fact, each part of the emitter is a whole new world with its own list of options to be tweaked. You can also add many other unique options to control the particle behaviors.

Keep in mind that working with particle systems requires an artist more than a programmer or coder. The only changes I made for the particle system was changing **Material** in the **Required** section to the one we made in the previous point. Set the **Use Local** Space to **true** in the **Required** section too, to force the particles emitter to update in the local space.

From the **Initial Size** section, I changed the **Max** and **Min** values to **20.0** rather than **25.0** as it fits more fruits.

Also, in the **Initial Velocity** section, I changed all of the **Z** values to negative rather than positive to force the particle to move down and not up.

Finally, I added a **curve** using the small curve button in the **Color Over Life** section. As the section name implies, that curve will be used to adjust the color over a lifetime. By changing the first and last points of each color curve, I was able to set its color to yellow with some sort of opacity.

Feel free to keep changing the values as the entire value name implies what they are and what they are going to affect. Also, feel free to add more than one emitter to generate more complex particle systems, but be aware that you are building for mobile devices, and particles need to be optimized!

Building the blueprints

Now is the time to start building the underlying logic for each blueprint, to have a gameplay logic that connects all of the game components together.

Player controller

You may have wondered why we are going to make this player controller. The answer is simple, to enable the ability to detect the swipe event (actually what looks like a swipe, not an actual swipe).

Right-click in your **Content Browser**, add a new blueprint, and select its base class to be **Player Controller**. I named it **fruitChopperPlayerController**. After adding a new blueprint, don't forget to submit it to the correct slot in the **Game Mode** blueprint that you make in each game.

Double-click on the newly created blueprint and from the **Defaults** tab, adjust the value of **Mouse Interface** to enable clicks and touches. Now the blueprints will be able to handle those events.

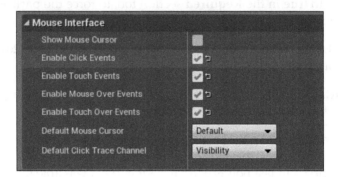

Fruits blueprints

I mentioned before that all of the fruits share the same logic, so in this step, I'll be showing you how to build one of the fruits, and then you can easily reconstruct or duplicate the rest of the fruits blueprints within a few seconds.

As we discussed how to build a multicomponent blueprint in *Chapter 3, Creating a Brick Breaking Game*, you need to make the fruit actor blueprint out of three components: the **Projectile Movement** component, the **Sphere** component as a collider, and the **PaperSprite** component, which will hold the art asset for the fruit. However, keep in mind that this time the **Projectile Movement** component should follow gravity, so make sure that **Projectile Gravity Scale** is set to **1.0**.

On **Event Begin Play**, you need to define that this blueprint can get even swipe inputs, so you need to add the **Enable Input** node and connect it to the **Get Player Controller** node. And since the game has only one player, you can leave **Player Index** set to **0** as it means the first player in the player array.

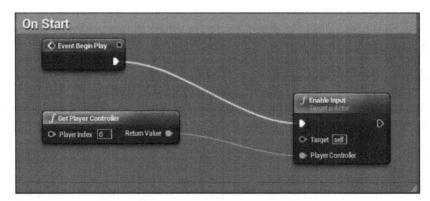

To interface a touch, get over the fruit (swipe); it is a little tricky. As the engine does not have swipe functionality right now, all we need is to just detect the moment when a finger moves over a fruit. So we will calculate it as a touch enter event by using the node **OnInputTouchEnter** or **EventTouchEnter** on later editor builds and set **FingerIndex** to **Touch 1** from the enum of touches.

If you were not able to find the enum of touches node, that means you are running a higher editor build. In that case, the easiest way to get a similar result is by looking for a node called **Equal(Byte)**, which is usually inside the **Byte** section of the **Math** node. This will give the same result but using numbers directly instead of enums.

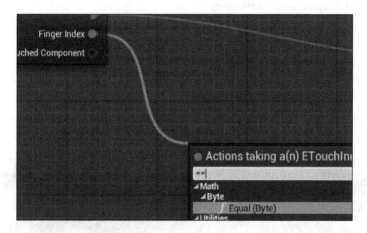

With this connection, perform the next step if the player has swiped over the current blueprint (which must have a collider and physics) with one finger. Then, you can add **Custom Event** and call it **Process Chopping,** and connect its call to **OnInputTouchEnter** and that emulates a successful swipe.

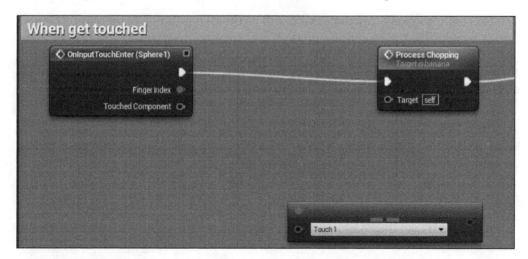

After calling **Process Chopping**, it is time to add to the score. If you haven't made a **fruitsGame** blueprint yet, go ahead and build an empty one with an empty **Custom Event** called **Add Score**, so that you can manage its call. Alternatively, you can add this part later when you finish adding the **fruitsGame** blueprint. There are so many ways to communicate between blueprints, and those ways are used according to the blueprint types. And as we are going to communicate between two normal blueprints that are based on the actor's class, the best way to do this is by searching and casting.

1. First, let's add a new variable of the type **fruitsGame_C**, which is the **fruitsGame** blueprint you have already made and left almost empty. Name it **fruitsGameManager**.

2. Then, you can use the **Get All Actors Of Class** node to look for all of the available actors of the selected **Actor Class** in the current level. Then, do a small **ForEachLoop** between them, and finally, run **Cast To fruitsGame** and apply the found one into the **fruitsGameManager** variable you created earlier.

3. Finally, call the **AddScore** function from the **fruitsGameManager** variable (which is the blueprint we found while using **Get All Actors Of Class**).

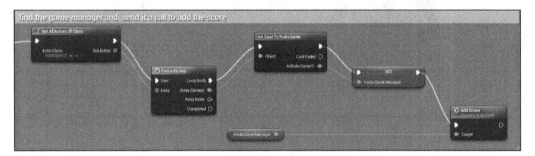

The **Process Chopping** function/event will be divided into two main parts. The first part is responsible for generating random and rotation positions to add the two new parts of the fruit based on the fruit's current position. The other part is responsible for adding the new sprites and destroying the full fruit sprite. Force the blueprint to stop receiving new inputs, so that we can hit a fruit once.

Using **Get Relative Location** to **PaperSprite** of the fruit, you can get its location. Then, using the returned data, you can generate new positions or rotations to the newly chopped sprites that you'll add. Make sure to use the **Random Float in Range**, **Make Rot**, **Vector+Vector**, and **Make Transform** nodes to construct randomization logic in your own style.

I forced the chopped pieces to be in almost the same positions (10 units to the left and right of the old sprite) and gave them a random rotation between **100** and **-100**.

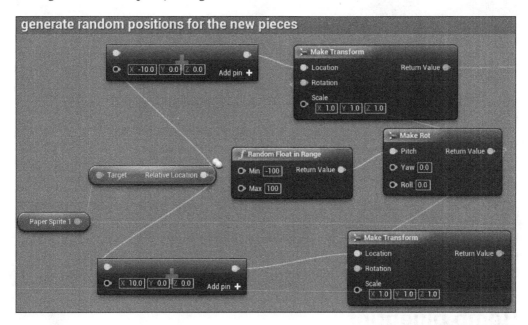

The last part of the fruit blueprint is adding and destroying the newly chopped parts. Using the node **Add PaperSpriteComponent**, you can add a new sprite. So using it twice will cause you to add two new sprites. Don't forget to set each of them to one of the two chopped pieces. Also, using the **Spawn Emitter at Location** node will allow you to drop a particle system emitter. Using **self** and **Get Actor Location** is a good idea to spawn the current position of the fruit.

Then, using **Destroy Component** and adding **PaperSprite** to its target will destroy the full fruit sprite and leave only two chopped pieces. Finally, to stop receiving events on this fruit blueprint (as it is already calculated in the score), you need to use **Unbind all Events from OnInputTouchEnter** and set the target to the **Sphere** collider (or whatever collider you are using as a physics component to the blueprint) and you will not receive any events again!

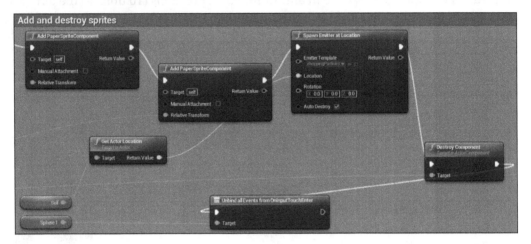

Now you can duplicate the blueprint to make all of the other fruits, but don't forget to change the sprites to the newly made fruit. Also, change the **Add PaperSpriteComponent** value to the correct value for chopped pieces.

Bomb blueprint

Most of the bomb logic is the same as any other fruit. So you can build and construct your components hierarchy in the same way. Or you can just duplicate one of the fruits and change its sprite to the bomb one.

You can keep only the start function from the old logic of a fruit, which is responsible for enabling the inputs. However, delete anything else related to chopping, as there will not be any chopping to the bomb.

Finally, you need to call the **Open Level** node when the player swipes over a bomb and sets its value to the **lose** level as **Level Name**. So it means that if the player swipes over the bomb, then open the lose level, which will contain a lose word.

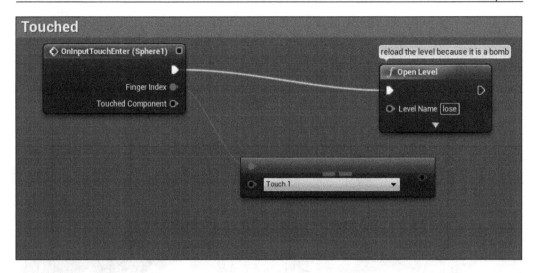

Win/lose blueprints

The **win** or **lose** blueprint will be used in a separate level file. Both of them have the same structure and logic; the only difference is in the text to be shown. So let's show you how to make one of them and you can make the other by duplicating it and changing the text value.

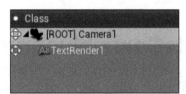

Create a new empty blueprint and name it **winScreen** and then add two components to it; a camera (orthographic one) and **TextRenderer**. Try to adjust the text position to fit the middle of the camera and then change its text value to a convenient phrase like **You Win**.

The last thing, in the blueprint logic, is that you need to set the camera component to be the correct one to render using the **Set View Target with Blend** node and run it in the **Event Begin Play** function with **Get Player Controller** as **Target** and keep **Player Index** as 0. Then, use a **Delay** node to wait for a duration of **2** seconds and then call the **Open Level** node and set **LevelName** to base, so the player gets into the gameplay again after two seconds. So either win or lose, the player sees the screen and after two seconds, he can go back to playing again.

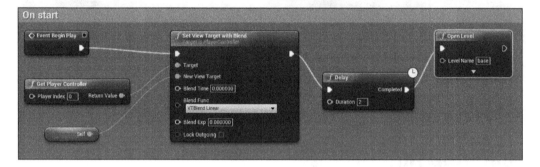

Now you can duplicate the blueprint, drop it in the **lose** level and change the text to **You Lose** and BOOM! You've created the lose screen in a second!

Don't forget to insert a directional light in the game level because the default UI will look black without a light source!

LevelLogic fruitsGame blueprint

The construction of the component hierarchy is very simple. You must have the **Camera** component that will render the game. And you need to have a **TextRenderer** that will work as the UI element to show the player score. And finally, you need several points in the space to be used as spawn points for the fruits; in my case, I made seven points, all of them are of the type **Billboard**.

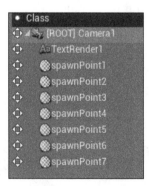

The final look of the blueprint when you drop a copy of it into the base level scene should look like this:

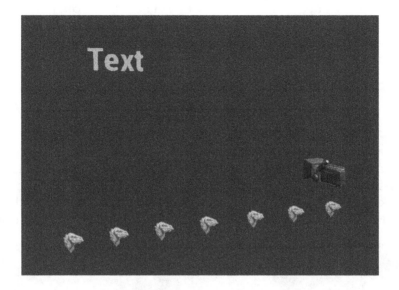

Before you start working on the logic part, you need to add several variables to be used during the process of building the gameplay logic. So add an **int** variable, call it **playerScore**. It is to be used as storage for the score value.

Add an integer called **instancesAmount** to be used as storage for the number of fruits that need to be spawned during the level. Add another integer called **instancingPoint**, which will work as a random value for the spawn point to be used for the current spawn operation. Another **int** called **fruitID** will be randomly changed, and its value will be used to randomly pick a fruit or bomb to be spawned. Finally, a **location** variable named **tempLocation** will be used to store the spawn point.

Now the last thing to be added before we start pitching the gameplay logic for this blueprint is something called Macro, which is a collapsed graph of nodes that have an entry point and exit point designated by tunnel nodes. You can find the add Macro button in the same tool bar you use to add a variable. Add a variable and name it `delayedLoop`. This one will be a normal for loop but will have a delay time before each iteration of the loop.

The easiest way to build it is by adding a normal for loop inside your graph and then double-clicking on it to access its **Macro**. Then, copy all of the components. Next, open the **delayedLoop** macro you made and paste everything. The only change you need to make is just add a **Delay** node to it before the **Sequence** node and give it a value. I found that a **Duration** value of **0.7** is working fine with the fruits shooting.

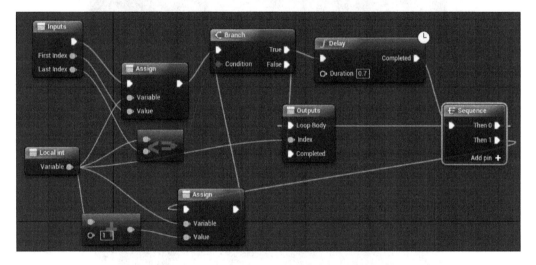

Now let's work on the logic. The first thing, as always, is **Event Begin Play**.

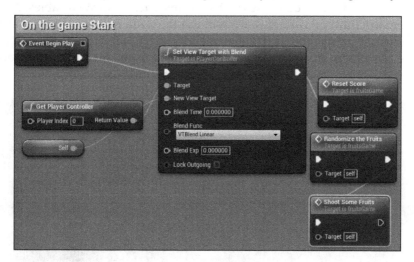

Let's add **Set View Target with Blend** to it to set the camera view to the current blueprint camera. Also, add **Get Player Controller** with **Player Index** of **0** to it to use the first player in the player's array.

- **Reset Score**: This is mainly used to set the score in the UI by setting the **playerScore** variable to zero (which is zero by default anyway), and converting it into **string** and applying it to the **TextRenderer** component using the **Set Tex** node and setting **Value** to the **playerScore** converted string.

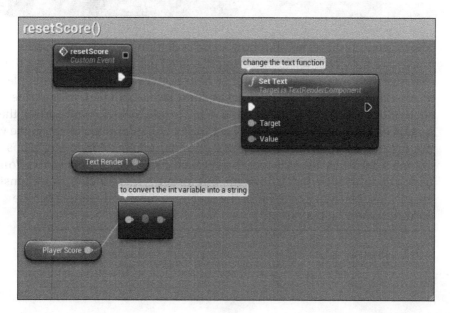

- **Randomize the Fruits**: This simple function will be called whenever we want to set a random value to the **fruitID** or **instancingPoint** variables. As both of them are **int** type variables, we will use the node **Random Integer in Range** and set the range for **fruitID** between **1** and **5** as all of the fruits and bombs are five blueprints only. Then set the range for **instancingPoint** to between **1** and **7** as I have only seven instances of the **billboard** components.

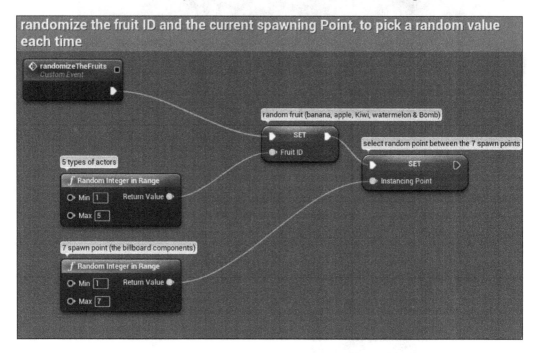

- **Shoot Some Fruits**: The first thing to do is defining how many fruit/ bombs we are going to shoot during this level using the **Set** node for the **instancesAmount** variable. I set it to **70** as it gives 4 minutes of gameplay approximately, which is not a long or short level. Using a `for` loop (the custom one we made which has the delay inside its logic) and adding the **instancesAmount** variable as its **Last Index** will guarantee us the game will fire the shot even for fruits with the same amount we defined. For loops are the best! Then call a custom event called **pickTheRandomSpawnPoint**, which I'll break down in a moment, but for now, this function is responsible for picking a spawn point out of the seven we have and using it for the current spawning operation.

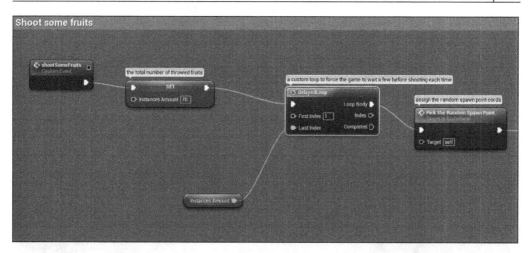

Finally, start executing several compare loops to check the random **fruitID** value. And according to the value, the blueprint will be spawning a different fruit blueprint using the **SpawnActor** node using **tempLocation** (we set its value in the **pickTheRandomSpawnPoint** function) as its spawn location.

Don't forget to assign a different fruit class to the **Class** value of the **SpawnActor** node. And note that I picked the number 5 of **fruitID** to represent the bomb actor blueprint.

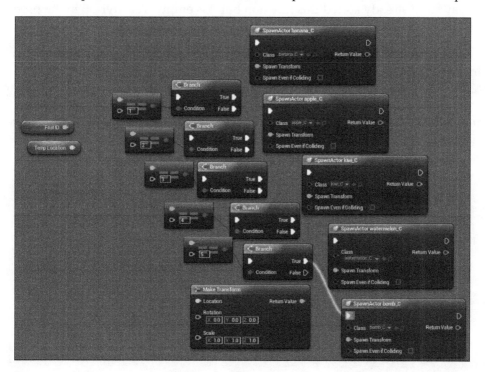

The **pickTheRandomSpawnPoint** event starts with a call to the **randomizeTheFruits** function, which was made to give a random **fruitID** and **instancingPoint**. Then, start to compare the variable **instancingPoint** to different values, and according to the compared value, we choose one of the **billboard** components positions to be the spawn point.

Then, by getting the location for the **billboard** point by the **Get World Location** node, we can get the value and store it to the **tempLocation** variable to be used in the rest of the spawning operation with the node Spawn Actor.

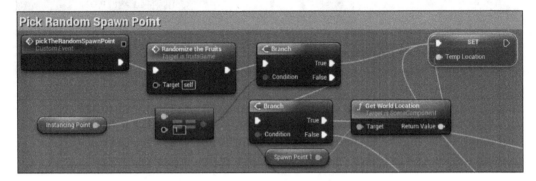

Now let's add the function that will be used to add the score to the layer. Remember you may have already added this function but it is empty. As advised in the process of creating a fruit blueprint, you may already have the **addScore** node type of custom event now.

Add a custom event and call it `addScore` if you haven't yet. Using the **Integer+Integer** node and applying the **playerScore** variable as one of its inputs and the value of **1** to the other input, you always get the value of 1 added to the latest score. By connecting the output of this calculation to a **Set** node of the **playerScore** variable and applying the result as a string to the **TextRenderer** node **SetText**, the score will be added and shown at the same time in the game UI.

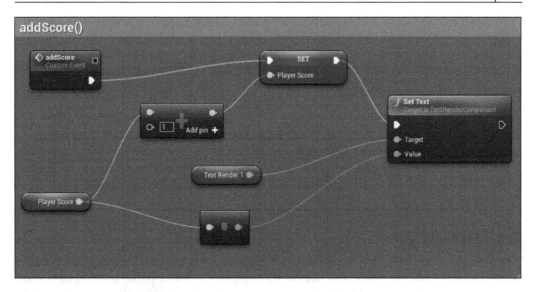

With the logic of showing a lose screen added to the bomb logic, we only have one case to break the game loop, which is the losing case. Now, it is time to add the logic for a win case.

By comparing the **playerScore** variable to **50** (the maximum for this level is 50 points) inside **Event Tick**, we can do whatever we want when the player hits 50. So using the **Open Level** node and setting its **Level Name** to the **win** level, we will be loading the win level once the player scores 50.

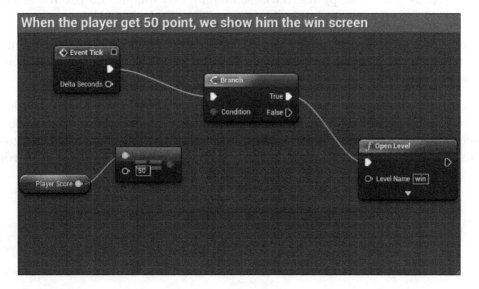

And now we have a full and complete game loop. The game starts and keeps running. If the player hits a bomb, it loads a lose screen and then waits for 2 seconds and takes them back into the game. If the player is skilled enough to avoid the bomb, once his score becomes 50, a win screen is loaded, which waits for 2 seconds, and then loads the game level again. And so on!

One last small note is that if you are still using the same version as I am, which is UE 4.3, you will not be able to see particles in the game. Don't panic! It is a known issue with the orthographic camera; if you switched the game camera to perspective, you'll be able to see the particles. This issue has been reported and it might be fixed with Version 4.5 or 4.6 as 4.4 is already out now, and it is not addressed it.

Summary

After you finished building your second iOS game with Unreal Engine, you probably started to feel at home inside the editor, started guessing and picking some new stuff that I never mentioned in this book, and became more familiar with the engine while building actual games.

Finishing this game gives you the chance to dig deeper into the editor's unique and powerful windows, such as the Cascade window for particles editing.

Also, you worked on building another material but with different properties and exploring a different shading mode than in the previous chapter.

Building your own for loop/macro was something very unique and you will start feeling its power when you start building more complex logic and projects.

Giving feedback to the user either with a UI score text or by displaying a different screen is something required nowadays within any successful game, and now you know how to do it.

Now it is time to build an even more complex game, with some collectables, basic enemies, and animations. If you feel that you already understand this chapter 100 percent, then you can start the next chapter; if not, then it is recommended that you go through this chapter once more, as the next game will be based on the knowledge you received in this chapter and *Chapter 3, Creating a Brick Breaking Game*.

5
Building an Exciting Endless Runner Game

Have you owned an iOS device? Or any other smartphone? If so, it means you have played at least five endless runner games. At the moment, the runners' genre is becoming a remarkable thing that distinguishes the smartphone devices from any other gaming platform out there. So learning how to make a runner game is something very important when it comes to learning about iOS game development with Unreal Engine. As the engine is well made and highly optimized, you will see how easy it will be to make a runner using Unreal Engine 4.x for iOS.

By the end of this chapter, you will be able to:

- Implement 2D sprite animations
- Learn about the basic tap controller
- Use the Character Controller class
- Build endless level logic
- Understand the importance of collectables
- Perform advanced communications between blueprints
- Pool the scene objects for better performance

The project structure

If you are going to see the already finished project that comes with this book, then you will find that it was made with Unreal Editor 4.30. If you are using a higher version, it might ask you that the project will be upgraded to a higher version, which is an undoable step. Just keep that in mind!

Since this game should have some sort of animation, I managed to build a character with a running animation, and also some items for the environment. Feel free to use your own handmade assets, or use the assets that come with this chapter's code or any other educational purposes. This chapter's code folder structure contains the following:

- **The Animations folder**: This contains two of the Paper2D flipbook animations.
- **The Blueprints folder**: This contains all of the blueprints (regardless of type).
- **The gameScene folder**: This holds only one level, which has the game in it.
- **The Materials folder**: This only contains one material which will be used for the font of the UI.
- **The Shapes folder**: This is the home for the basic 3D shapes that were used to block the level.
- **The Sprites folder**: This is the home for all of the textures and sprites. It contains the main textures and the generated sprites.

Importing the assets

In case you decide to start working with the provided assets from scratch (or maybe with your own unique assets), with this chapter's files you will find a folder called `pngAssets` with one other subfolder and a few other PNG files inside the main directory.

Select all of the images inside the `png` folder and then drag and drop them inside the **Content Browser** window of your Unreal Editor as discussed in *Chapter 4, Advanced Game Content Generation with a Fruit Chopper Game,* and keep going in the same process of converting those texture images into Paper2D sprites to be used in the game. Textures can be used only to show an object surface while displaying a material, but sprites can be used as independent flat objects.

Building the animated sprites

Right-click inside **Content Browser**. Choose the **Sprite Flipbook** type from within the **Animation** submenu and you'll be able to add an empty animated sprite to your project directory.

Double-click on this new asset to open its proper animation editor, which looks like (and is actually) a very simple and easy-to-use editor.

To keep the animations as simple as possible, I managed to build only two:

- **Idle animation**: This will be displayed when the player is in the air
- **Running animation**: This will be displayed as long as the player is on the ground

By selecting all of the frames from the **Sprites** folder and dragging them into the lower-left corner of the animation editor, you can place them into this animated sprite. Now you'll be able to see a live view of the frames playing.

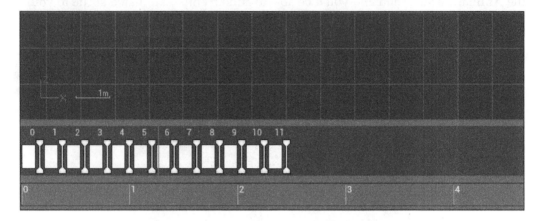

As these animations have been made in 24 FPS (every second of animation is made of 24 * .png images), you'll need to adjust this property inside the right panel of the animation editor. Also, this panel will show you the total number of frames this sprite is made of (12 frames).

The other animated sprite (the flying/idling one) is very simple, as you can pick one frame only and put it inside a new animated sprite. As the character should not do too many actions while flying in the air, a one frame animation will get the job done. I picked frame number 3 as both of the legs were straight!

An overview of blueprints

As the game has only four blueprints, which sounds like a small number for such a game, all of them build the logic behind this complex endless game type. In fact, only two blueprints do all of the game logic and the other two were made for organization purposes. The following are the four blueprints:

- **runnerMode**: This is the **Game Mode** blueprint type for this game, and as mentioned earlier, it is very important to have different game modes per level or per game.

- **levelLayout**: This is an **Actor** blueprint type and it contains the level construction, the laser beams, the collectables, the UI, and the logic for the endless running, and score calculations.

- **madScientist**: This is from a **Character** blueprint type, which contains the animated sprites and the logic for the input and collisions with the laser beams and collectables.

- **madScientistController**: This is from a **Player Controller** blueprint type, which was necessary to work with the **Character** blueprint and to enable the mouse/touch events.

The gameplay mechanics

As mentioned with the previous game in *Chapter 4, Advanced Game Content Generation with a Fruit Chopper Game* instead of explaining the mechanism of the gameplay loop it will be better for you to work from scratch or to understand the current logic you got with the book. With that said, let's break down the gameplay logic:

1. Once the game starts and as long as the score is less than 100; the **levelLayout** blueprint will keep moving the **Blocks** transform towards the left to give the appearance of a running level. Once the **Blocks** transform reaches its endpoint (completes showing the last block) the **levelLayout** blueprint will reset the position of the **Blocks** transform and show the collectables, to start displaying the level continually again.

2. The **madScientist** blueprint, which is the player, will start receiving the inputs from the touchscreen or the keyboard/mouse. As long as the player is running on the ground, the animated sprite will display a running loop animation; otherwise, it will display the idle animation. If the player hits a collectable item, it will force this collectable item to disappear and then add one point to the score by calling its function in the **levelLayout** blueprint. However, if the player hits a laser beam, it will restart the level.

Building the blueprints

As mentioned with the previous game in *Chapter 4, Advanced Game Content Generation with a Fruit Chopper Game*, explaining the mechanism of the gameplay loop, it will be better for you to work from scratch or understand the current logic you got with the book. With that said, let's breakdown the gameplay logic:

- **madScientistController**: Build a new blueprint of type **Player Controller** and set all of its **Mouse Interface** options to **True**, because as mentioned earlier in *Chapter 2, Methods and Tools to Create Your Games*, we will be using the mouse events to simulate touch events.

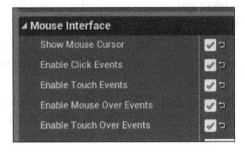

- **madScientist**: Build a new **Character** class blueprint and you will find that it has several components by default:

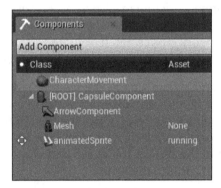

The components under the character class are as follows:

- ° **CharacterMovement**: This is the component responsible for all of the movement and physics of the character. Feel free to explore the vast number of variables inside this component, but the default values will work best for this example.

- ° **CapsuleComponent**: This is the Capsule collider that works with the movement component as the main body mass.

- ° **Arrow Component**: This is a simple component to define the direction the player is facing.

- ° **Mesh**: This is the component that should hold the player mesh. And as we don't have a 3D mesh for the player (the game is 2D), you can keep this mesh component as it is (empty) or you can delete it if you wish.

You will need to add a **Paper Flipbook** component and pick the running animation to be the default animation for it. So you get the player sprite displayed. You might need to scale it down to **0.4** as the sprite was made in HD resolution. Or you can scale up **Capsule Component**. Do as you like. Also, rotating it by 90 degrees on the Z-axis is a good way to have it facing in the right direction.

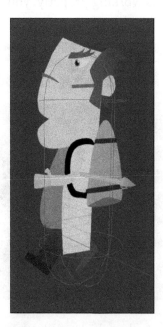

- **runnerMode**: Build a **Game Mode** class type and assign it to the level as usual to host the level mode. However, since we have a **Character** type class to control the player this time, you will be assigning it to the **Default Pawn Class** option, and keeping all of the other variables as before.

To make sure this one is working properly, you will need to insert a **Player Start** actor into the scene.

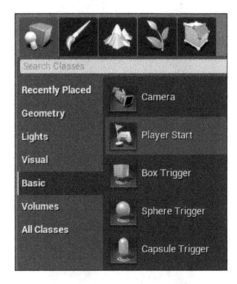

The way it works is that when the level starts, as long as **Player Start** is in the scene, it will spawn the player class (the **Character** class) that you used as the default pawn class inside the active game mode.

- **levelLayout**: This blueprint is very similar to the one you made in *Chapter 3, Creating a Brick Breaking Game*. So you will be adding a camera, four walls to block the level layout, a UI text to host the score, and several transform points (**Billboard**) to work as the parent for the collectables and laser beams (the level components). One thing you want to make sure is that the level is built on blocks; each block is a parent for several sprites. And all of those blocks are children of one giant transform called **Blocks** (the one we will move during the gameplay).

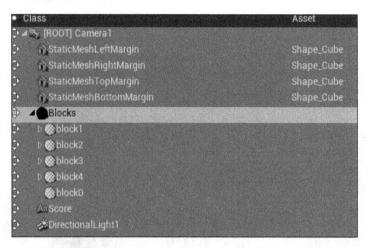

- Don't forget to add the **collectable** tag to all of the collectables, and the **laser** tag to all of the laser beams. Also, mark **Collision Presets** as **OverlapAll** for both of them (collectables and laser objects). I made only four blocks, but you can make as many blocks as you wish, and keep in mind that more blocks will give more variations to the game!

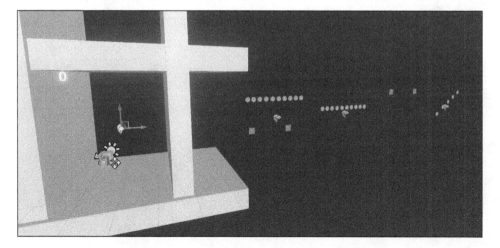

Building the logic

As you may have noticed while building the blueprints, the only two blueprints that can possibly hold logic were the **Character** type blueprint called **madScientist** and the **Actor** type blueprint called **levelLayout**. The first one will hold the logic for the controller and anything related to the player, while the second will hold the logic for the level movement/generation of collectables and score updating.

- On **Event Begin Play**, I will be using **View Target With Blend** to set the current camera view as the main camera for this level.

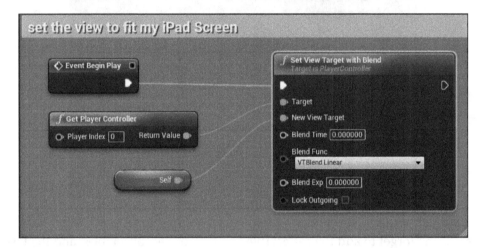

- Then, add a custom event called **addScore** to be the one that will control the **Collectables Score** variable of type **int** that holds the score result. Next, use the resultant final score to be displayed by the UI **Score** text object using the **Set Text** node and pass the **Collectables Score** value as a string using the **Int to String conversion** node.

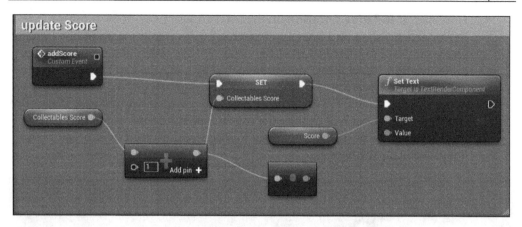

- Now on the **Tick** event, which takes place in every frame, we will be checking whether the **Collectables Score** value is less than **100** or not. Because if the value is more than **100**, I'll consider the player victorious and then play the level again using the **Open Level** node (or show a win screen as in *Chapter 4, Advanced Game Content Generation with a Fruit Chopper Game*). However, if the player's score is still less than **100**, it means the level should keep running by checking whether the **Blocks** parent transform **Relative Location** on the Y-axis is more than **-3400** (which is the full loop of the four blocks the level is made of).

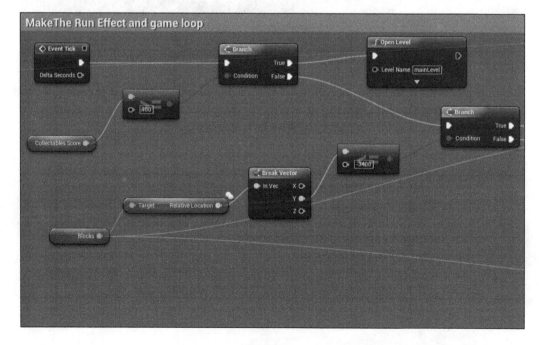

- However, if **Relative Location** on the y axis is less than **-3400**, it means that the level is finished and I need to reset the position to the default one (which was **0** on the Y-axis), show all of the collectables again using a custom event called **Show Collectables,** and finally, start moving the level again using **Add Relative Location** and adding a small value to the Y-axis. I managed to make a float variable for this small value and called it **Runner Speed** because changing this value will change the overall speed of the level, and it can be used later for game design purposes to increase the speed over time or over the player's performance.

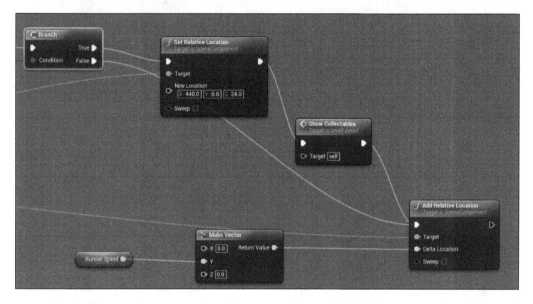

However, if **Relative Location** on the y axis value is not less, it means the camera is still showing new parts to the player, so I keep using **Add Relative Location** to move the **Blocks** transform object.

- The **Show Collectables** event is very simple, as I used a reference to all of the collectables I have in the level and applied a node called **Set Visibility** to them and marked its **New Visibility** variable to **True**. Now I make sure that when the level starts to loop, it will reset the visibility of the collected items to show them again and again make them available to be collected. (The pooling theory for better performance in *Chapter 8, iOS Debugging and Optimization*). We can also use a `for` loop during runtime to look for those collectables and reset them, but having a reference for them before starting the level is a faster way than looking for them during runtime.

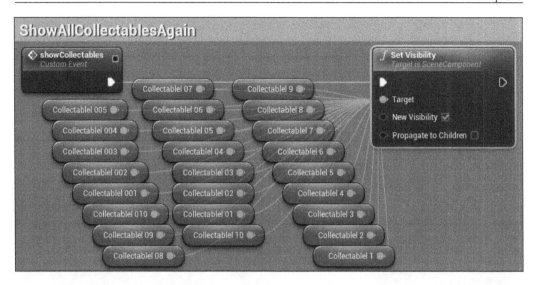

- Using the **Space Bar** actions and the **Input Touch** actions is the easiest way to set up a controller for the game quickly. As the game does not require on screen joysticks, or for the player to tap on a specific area, both of those functions will work fine to simulate the player pressing or tapping the screen. And as we are using the **Character** class to control the player's character, we have direct access to a function called **Jump**, which will cause the player to jump with the specified force in the **Movement component**.

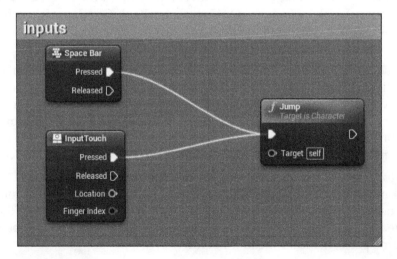

- On **Event Tick**, we can check every frame to know whether the **Character Movement** component of the **Character** class is moving on the ground, and using the returned Boolean value to control whether we will display a running animation or in air idle animation. Using the **Set Flipbook** node, we can easily control which animation is displayed for which **Target** flipbook animated component.

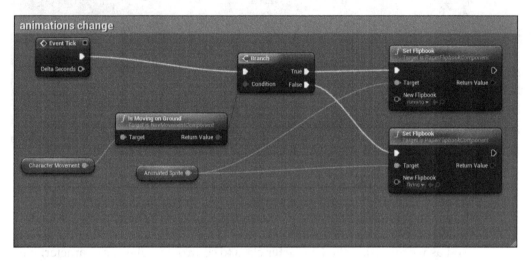

- To be able to detect overlap events with the other components of other actors (the collectables and laser are components of the **levelLayout** actor blueprint), you will use the **OnComponentBeginOverlap** node, which is meant to detect the overlap of other actors or components with the current component, that is, the **CapsuleComponent** in this case.

- I used two **Branch** nodes (if statements) to detect whether the overlap was with **Component Has Tag** of **collectable** or **Component Has Tag** of **laser**. And based on the result, I execute several steps. If **Component Has Tag** of **laser**, I will use an **Open Level** node to reopen the level again, or in other words, restart the level (you can also show a lose screen as we did in *Chapter 4, Advanced Game Content Generation with a Fruit Chopper Game*).

  However, if **OnComponentBeginOverlap** has overlapped with **Component Has Tag** of **collectable**, then I'll set the visibility of the other component (the collectable) to **False** (to hide it. I don't like the idea of destroying an instantiating object as it is never a good idea for game performance; we call it Pooling.)

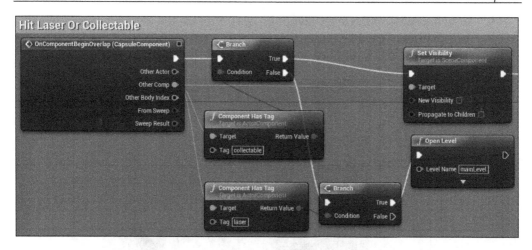

- After hiding the collectable item, it is time to add points to the score in order to reward the player. Therer is a custom event called **Add Score** inside the **levelLayout** blueprint, which is responsible for adding the score, so to be able to call this blueprint, we have to search for it first and then give the call.

- Using **Get All Actors Of Class**, we can get a reference to all of the actor classes inside the current level. And as we use the **levelLayout** class one time only inside the level, it will return an array of one element only. By casting a variable called **Level Manager**, we can save that returned reference and then call the **Add Score** function on it.

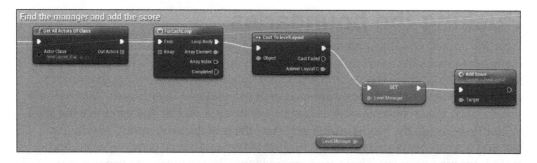

- Now if you drop the levelLayout blueprint inside the level view, and tweak the position of the Player Start element, you have a fully functional endless runner level. Click on **Play** or deploy to a device, it's up to you.

Pushing the boundaries

Now the game looks like a normal runner, but you can still add other game design elements to make the game more fun and give it more user interaction. For example, you can add sound effects or particles as we explained in the previous chapters, or add some more obstacle types, animated ones or animated laser beams. Alternatively, you can add more collectable types and power ups. Or maybe you can force the level to shuffle between the blocks and never show them in the same order. Maybe you can add a small missions system to force the player to achieve some missions and tasks from his gameplay. There are so many game design ideas you can use, but game design is a different topic than the target of this book.

Summary

While building your third iOS game with Unreal Engine, you got involved with lots of new stuff. As you started to build 2D animations, you got familiar with the Paper2D flipbook animation editor. Also, you started to use the Character class, which is one of those amazing and powerful features of Unreal Engine. All games have player/character controllers, and getting your hands on this class will save you lots of time in the future from writing custom classes or building custom controller logic. The character class comes with an engine that is very powerful and optimized.

Also, you got rough ideas about how to make a pooling system to keep reusing items or objects in the scene rather than destroying them and instantiating new ones during runtime.

Now, after perfectly understanding the player controller and the collectables, it is time to make even more complex games. In the next chapter, you will be working in an advanced way with the player controller, collectables, basic enemies, and projectiles.

6
Designing an Advanced Game

Want to make even more complex games? Want to have a more complex controller and not just a tap all over the screen? What about a platformer? Move, navigate, jump, and fire some bullets to kill enemies.

In this chapter, you will be running through the process of building a platformer level with a more advanced player controller with touch interface inputs, more complex actors, and new components.

By the end of this chapter you will be able to:

- Use the 2D colliders
- Use the touch interface to add on-screen buttons
- Add some enemies and make them responsive
- Add projectiles on runtime as bullets
- Use an actor as a component
- Randomly spawn enemy types
- Pass custom inputs into custom events

The project structure

If you are going to use the already finished project that comes with the book, then you will find that it was made with the Unreal Editor 4.3. If you are using a higher version, it might ask you to upgrade the project to a higher version, which is an irreversible step. Just keep this in mind!

You encountered the main character of this game in the last chapter, but there are also some new items for the environment. Feel free to use your own handmade assets or use the assets that come with this example for the chapter or any other educational purpose. This chapter's folder structure contains the following:

- **The Blueprints folder**: This contains all of the blueprints used to build this game logic

- **The Flipbooks folder**: This contains all five flipbook animations used in the game

- **The Frames folder**: This contains all of the textures and sprites used for the animations, the background, and the environment items.

- **The Maps folder**: This holds one level, which is the game.

- **The Materials folder**: This contains one material which is used with the level blocking.

- **The StarterContent folder**: This is the home for the basic 3D shapes that you might need to use.

- **The UIButtons folder**: This contains the textures used to build the touch interface.

Importing the assets

In case you decide to start working from scratch with the provided assets (or maybe with your own unique assets), with this chapter's files you will find a folder called **pngAssets** with other subfolders that are named with the proper asset or animation name with PNG files inside them.

Select all of the images inside the **png** folder and then drag and drop them inside the **Content Browser** window in your Unreal Editor as discussed in *Chapter 4, Advanced Game Content Generation with a Fruit Chopper Game*.

Keep on converting those texture images into Paper2D sprites to be used in the game as textures can only be used to show an object surface while displaying a material, but sprites can be used as independent flat objects.

Building the animated sprites

After right-clicking inside the **Content Browser** window you can choose the **Sprite Flipbook** type from within the **Animation** submenu to be able to add an empty animated sprite to your project directory.

Double-click on this new asset to open the sprites animation editor, which is a very simple and easy-to-use editor.

To keep the animations as simple as possible, I built only five of them:

- **enemyGreen**: This is the main and only animation for the green type of enemy creature.
- **enemyRed**: This is the main and only animation for the red type of enemy creature.
- **scientistIdle**: This is the idle animation for the player character that will be used while there are no inputs.
- **scientistShoot**: This is the animation that will be used when the player presses the fire button.
- **scientistWalk**: As in the previous chapter, this animation will be used while there is a horizontal movement input.

By selecting all of the frames from the **Sprites** folder and dragging them, as we did in *Chapter 5, Building an Exciting Endless Runner Game*, into the lower-left corner of the animation editor, you can place them into this animated sprite and you'll be able to see a live view of the frames playing.

Some of these animations have been made at 24 FPS, and others at 15 FPS; you'll need to adjust this property in the right-hand side panel of the animation editor, so remember to ask your animator about the frame rate used.

The blueprints

As this game is at a relatively larger scale than all of the other games we have created up until now, you will find that the game contains even more blueprints. With this project, you will find nine blueprints, which are defined as follows:

- **bullet**: This is a blueprint based on the actor class that represents a bullet projectile to be spawned when the player shoots an enemy.
- **crateBox**: This is a blueprint based on the actor class that represents the collectable items all over the level to fill the player's weapon with ammo.
- **enemyGreen**: This is a blueprint based on the actor class that has a basic logic for the enemy to navigate through the level.
- **enemyRed**: This is a blueprint based on the actor class that has a basic logic for the enemy with a different flipbook animation to navigate through the level.

- **gameInputs**: This is a blueprint based on the touch interface class that holds the necessary on-screen buttons.

- **mainChar**: This is a blueprint based on the Character class that contains the player controller.

- **shootingGameMode**: This is a blueprint based on the Game Mode class that is used as the game mode for this level.

- **spawnPoint**: This is a blueprint based on the actor class that has a basic logic for spawning of random enemies.

- **uiText**: This is a blueprint based on the actor class that has only the UI text. As this game have more text to display, I decided to split it into its own blueprint.

The gameplay mechanic

As mentioned in the previous game, explaining the mechanism of the gameplay loop will be better for you if you plan to work from scratch or to understand the current logic you've got with the book. With this said, let's break down the gameplay logic:

1. Once the game starts, all of the **spawnPoint** blueprints in the scene will keep spawning random enemy types as long as the player never reaches the targeted score or is still alive.

2. The **mainChar** blueprint will be able to receive inputs from the keyboard and the touch screen as long as the game is running. Once the player hits jump, this action will force the player controller to jump, while hitting fire will force him to stop and shoot some bullet blueprints.

3. While shooting, the player's amount of ammo keeps decreasing while the score increases if the bullets hit some enemies, and both are displayed through the **uiText** blueprint.

4. Finally, if the player falls through a gap or touches an enemy, the level will restart; whereas, if the player hits a **cratebox** blueprint, it will add 10 extra bullets to the amount of ammo the player has.

Building the blueprints

As almost everything taking place in the game should be made using the blueprints, it is time to start working on the blueprints based on their importance for the correct construction of the gameplay loop:

gameInputs

As briefly described earlier, this blueprint will be responsible for the integration of the touch interface. It should be the first blueprint made, so that we can make use of this input with the player. The touch interface, by default, copies its events from a keyboard or controller binding; this means that we have to figure out some inputs in **Project Settings** for the keyboard, and then we will map it to the touch interface.

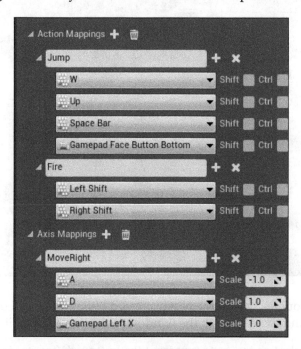

As you can see, I've added a **Jump**, **Fire**, and **MoveRight** movement to **Input**. Feel free to assign any buttons to these movements that make you happy on the controller. However, remember that these bindings will be used with the touch interface.

Now that you can create a touch interface blueprint; right-click on your **Content Browser** window, select **Miscellaneous**, and finally select **Touch Interface Setup**. This will add a purple-colored blueprint icon. Feel free to name it whatever you want, in my case it is called **gameInputs**.

Now when you double-click on the newly created blueprint, it will open the touch interface setup window. Although the window looks very simple, it is very powerful.

You just need to select an image to represent the button, define its size, and its position, and finally define which buttons it should simulate. In the first case, I chose the **buttonFire** art asset to simulate the **Left Shift** or **Right Shift** button clicks, which were introduced in the **Input** tab of **Project Settings** as Fire input in **Action Mappings**. Now it is your turn to keep adding buttons and following the same process as my current game inputs have. What do you think about adding a pause button?

Finally, it is time to force these buttons to appear on the screen. Up until this moment, the buttons are not displayed or accessible. To achieve this, you need to navigate to **Project Settings** again, select the **Input** tab, and finally from the **Mobile** section, you need to set the blueprint you made to the **Default Touch Interface** option.

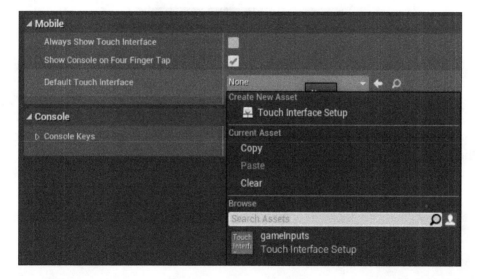

uiText

To show the titles, I used two text components and set one of them to display **Ammo** and the other to display **Score**.

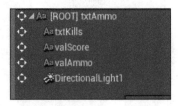

Then, I added two other text components to display the values themselves, which are **0** right now.

Finally, I added a directional light as we have done earlier to show the text in the scene view.

In the graph view, I've added two integer variables (which are **ammo** and **score**) to store and control the UI values.

mainChar

The character has the same structure as the player character in *Chapter 5, Building an Exciting Endless Runner Game*, but this time I've added a new **Child Actor** component type rather than putting the UI to the camera. I prefer to show a new way to set the UI which is more efficient. Now you can assign the **uiText** blueprint actor to a child component of the **mainChar** blueprint.

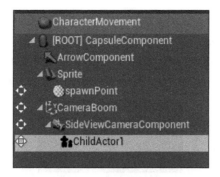

Also, I've added a **billboard** component to represent the point from which I'm going to spawn the bullet.

Finally, I added a **bullet** integer variable into the graph to help me store and check the current ammo the player has, to prevent the bullets from spawning if the player keeps pressing while his ammo is empty.

enemyRed

Do you remember how we managed to build our **projectile** components in the fruits game? The same magical component will work efficiently in building these kinds of simple enemies.

Using just a **projectile** component, **paper Flipbook**, and **Sphere collider**, I was able to build an entire enemy.

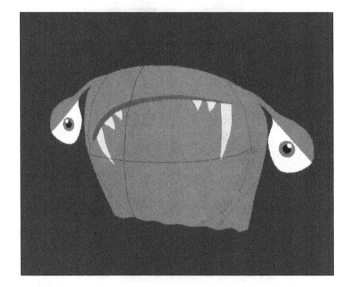

Just remember that I've made some tweaks to the **projectile** component to alter its behavior to match what I had in mind. Set **initial speed** to **120**, activate **Should Bounce**, reduce **Bounciness** to a very low value such as **0.1**, disable **Friction** by setting it to **0.0**, and finally give it a velocity of **200** on the *X*-axis as this represents the horizontal movement.

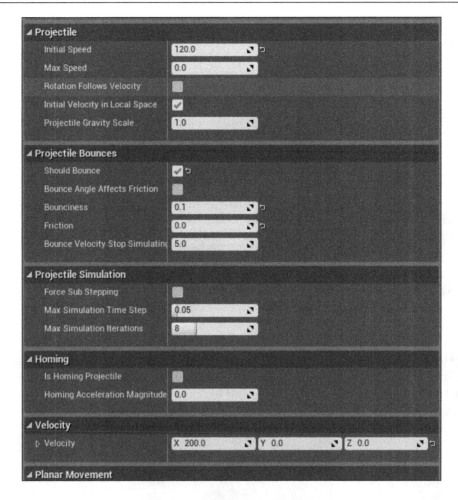

Finally, setting the **sphere** component to **Simulate Generate Hit Events** and **Generate Overlap Events** while giving it an **enemy** tag will give you easy access to control its effects on the environment.

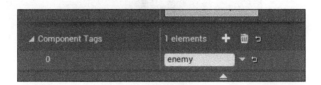

With a fully finished enemy in hand, you can now duplicate it to make the **greenEnemy** blueprint, but this time, use the green enemy animations. Later when you build a one-enemy logic, it's just a matter of copying and pasting it to the nodes to make the other enemy work fine.

crateBox

This is the simplest blueprint in the game. It is just a **paper2d** component with its own collider.

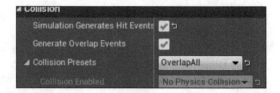

It has its physics component set to **Simulate Generate Hit Events** and **Generate Overlap Events** while having a **crate** tag.

bullet

This is a typical projectile construction, like the enemy, but this time **Projectile Gravity Scale** has been set to **0.0** to prevent the bullets from falling to the ground and the **velocity** has been set to **400** to force them to move fast.

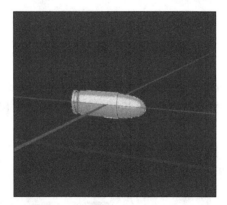

It still has its physics set to **Simulate Generate Hit Events** and **Generate Overlap Events** but its tag is set to **bullet**.

shootingFGameMode

Now, after getting a player character controller blueprint, you can quickly set up the game mode. The only unique option I was setting was the **Default Pawn Class** to use my **mainChar** blueprint.

spawnPoint

The spawn point is made of just one component, which is a billboard. I added it to have a point in space, and nothing more. The only other thing I've added was a variable called **randomValue**, which I'll be using to randomly select to spawn a green or red enemy.

Building the logic

Now it is time to put everything together and start building the connections between all of the blueprints. In fact, it is easier than it looks like, and with that in mind, let's start.

uiText

To change the score value, I've added a custom event and called it **setScore**. This custom event will be working on setting the value of the **Score** variable by adding **1** to it using the **integer + integer** node. The final result of the score value will be displayed in the UI using the **Set text** node. Keep in mind that you can use whatever values you want, as long as you are using the **add** node. This node will be working on adding the first passed integer value to the second passed integer.

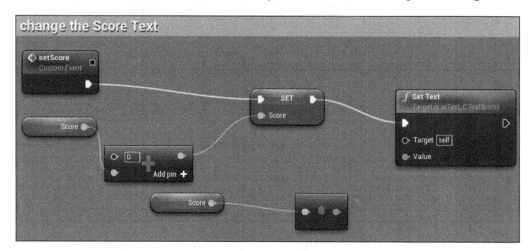

I wanted to follow a new method to change the value of ammo, which is closer to the code environment that I have used over the years. It is called passing parameters. Basically, when I called an event or function, I wanted to send the exact new value directly to it, and then use it to set the ammo text based on the passed parameter. To add this type of parameter passing, I've added a new custom event, called it **setAmmo**, and after selecting the node in the side panel, I've added a new input to **Inputs**, set its type to **Integer**, and set its name to **ammoAmount**. Now any call to this event will require passing an integer value, otherwise it will use the default which, is set to **0** for now.

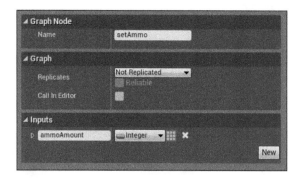

Finally, I used the passed ammo value from the **AmmoAmount** parameter and set it as a string to the **Set text** node, to change the proper UI text.

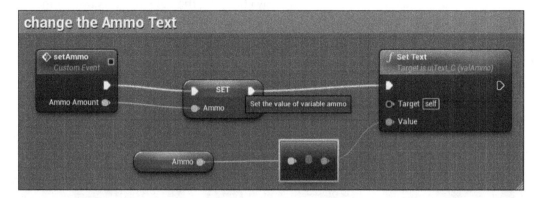

enemyRed

I've added two rectangles in the scene to represent walls and gave them a **wall** tag. Then, I started using **OnComponentHit** that is caused by the **sphere** component of the enemy blueprint.

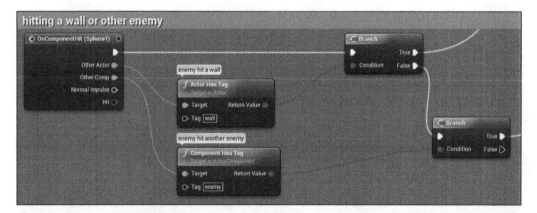

We check whether the enemy hit a **wall** tagged actor with the **Actor Has Tag** node, or another **enemy** tagged component with the **Component Has Tag** node. If yes, then the enemy changes its movement direction by changing the **velocity** direction of the **projectile** component and changing **scale** of **sprite** between **1** and **-1** to emulate a flip.

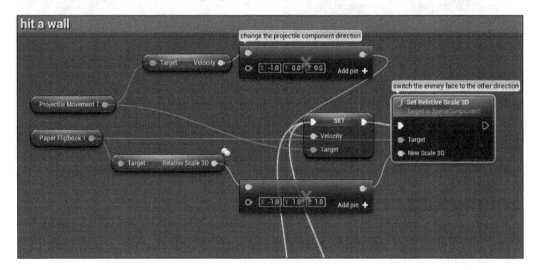

spawnPoint

Using the **Spawn Actor Of Class** node on **Event Begin Play**, I was able to spawn enemies. However, to ensure that it is random and lasts for a while, I set a random value to the **RandomValue** variable and based on the resulting value, I pick whether to spawn a red or green enemy.

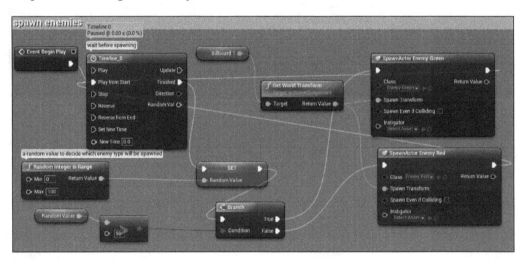

To ensure that it is sort of a loop, I decided to use a new approach, which is the **Timeline** node. This node controls a value over time. I set its time in its graph to 1.5 seconds, and never cared about the resulting value as I won't be using it, I just madee use of the animation duration and forced it to run every time an enemy finishes spawning. With this, I get the following sequence:

1. Execute the timeline node.
2. The node finishes running.
3. Randomize the value of the integer.
4. Select an enemy type.
5. Spawn the enemy.
6. Run the timeline node.

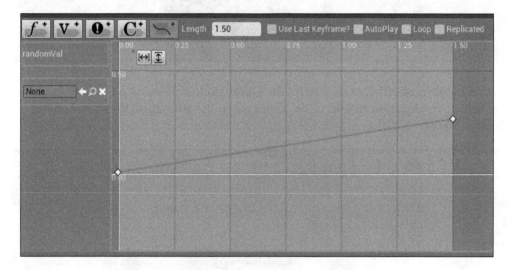

bullet

As the **Delay** node is broken for my current version of Unreal Engine, I had to find a way to ask the bullet to wait for a while after it is spawned and then destroy itself.

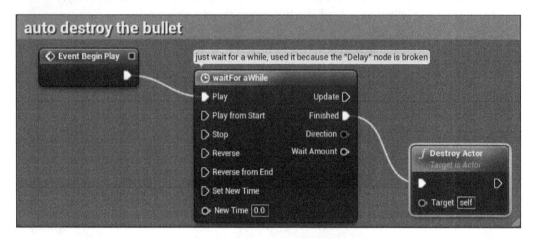

The best and most efficient way to fix the **Delay** node was using a **timeline** node and setting its duration to **4** seconds. Then, when the animation finished, I called **Destroy Actor**.

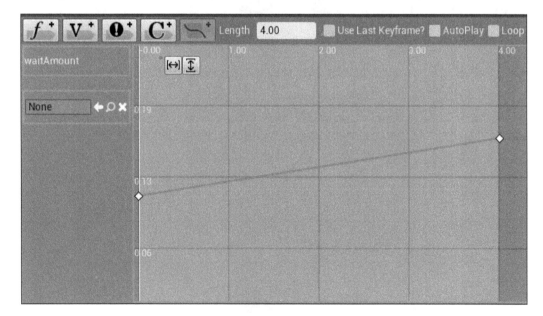

The rest of the calculations of the bullet were done using **OnComponentBeingOverlap** and checking the overlapped components.

If the overlapped component had an **enemy** tag then I just called **Destroy actor** to destroy the parent actor that holds this component. Finally, I used a quick search method such as **Get All Actors Of Class** to look for the **uiText** class and called its **setScore** custom event to add **1** to the score and the UI.

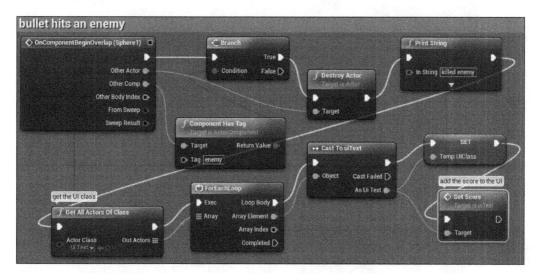

mainChar

With a custom event named **changeAmmoValue**, I started looking for **uiTextClass** using the same **Get All Actors Of Class** as before and then calling the **SetAmmo** event. However, as we have set up this event in a way that requires it to pass an integer value, I passed the value of the local variable bullets to it.

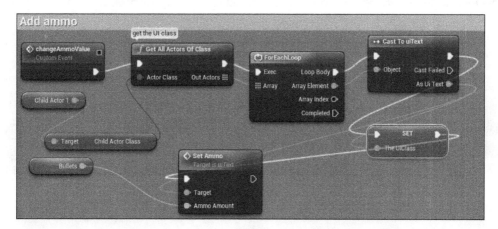

By calling **changeAmmoValue** on **Event Begin Play**, I was assured that every time the level is started, the UI will be updated to the default value of the local variable bullets.

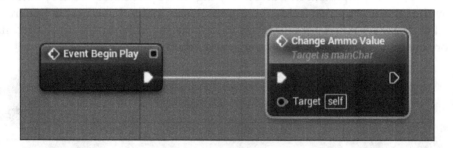

Due to the usage of a character-based blueprint, I was able to simply simulate a jump by calling the **Jump** or **Stop jump** function on the controller when I had to.

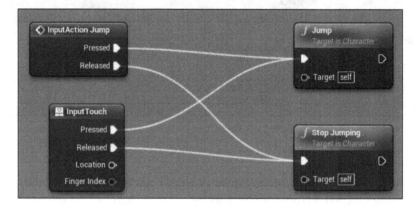

To ensure that the player can't just shoot continuously, we check the value of the local variable bullets before processing a bullet spawning process. Every time the player presses the shoot button, we make sure that the number of bullets is more than **0** and then call the **shoot** event to process a bullet and call the **changeAmmoValue** to reduce the number of bullets.

The **shoot** event itself is just using the **spawnPoint** type of **billboard** component to get a world transform and then using the **Spawn Actor of Class** node to spawn the **bullet** blueprint.

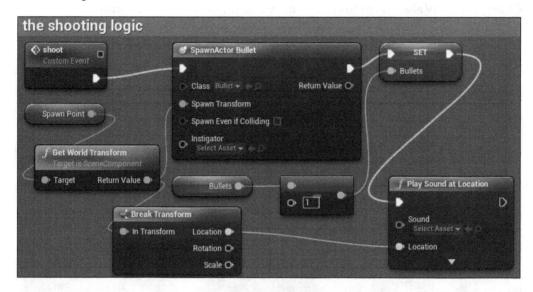

Then it reduces the total number of the current bullets in the local variable **bullets** by 1 using the **integer – integer** node, and finally plays a shooting sound at the location of the spawning.

In case the character controller **Event Hit** gets hit with a component that has an **enemy** tag, then the level needs to be restarted as the player will die.

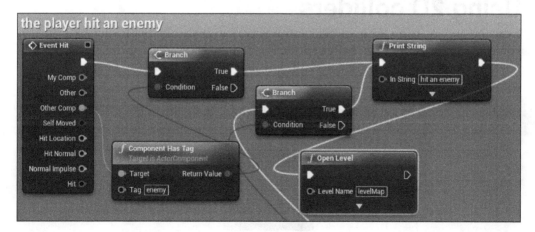

However, if the **Capsule** component of the character controller has been overlapped with a crate that is a tagged component, then I use **Destroy Actor** to destroy the **crate** blueprint actor instance, add **10** to the **bullet** local variable, and call the **ChangeAmmoValue** event to change the value on the **uiText** blueprint.

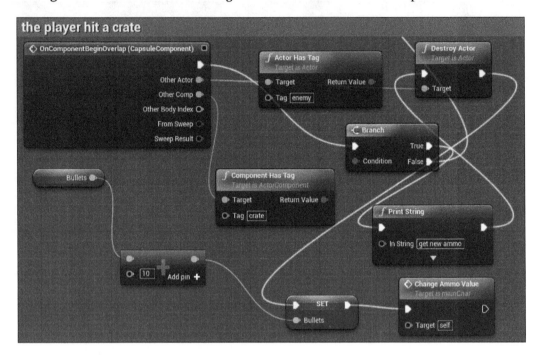

Using 2D colliders

Now the only missing thing in this platform is, obviously, the platform itself. As you can see, the project has a **tiles** sprite. It is not an actor, it is a sprite, but it has a physics component inside it by default. You can remove, update, or change what it looks like.

Double-click on it to get access to the sprites editor, navigate to the top button bar, and select the **Edit Collision** button that will bring you into the collisions mode.

This will enable a new button on the top bar. Using the newly activated **Add Polygon** button, you can keep adding new polygons to the collision mesh, or you can remove by simply hitting *Delete* on the keyboard.

While editing, you will see that the viewport is updating you in real time, and it will feel more like a 3D poly edit application such as Maya or 3DsMax.

Once you're finished, don't forget to make sure of the collision settings, and as this sprite will be used as a platform to stand on, you can simply set **Collision Preset** to **Block All Dynamics**, and **Collision Thickness** to a high number to make sure no assets fall into the background while platforming.

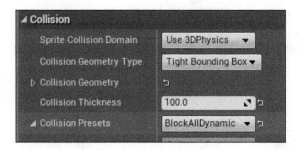

Pushing the boundaries

Now, with all of the components of the level, you can simply drag and drop items into the scene to construct a level from your imagination. You can add more flavor to it; you can start building custom particle systems as discussed in *Chapter 4, Advanced Game Content Generation with a Fruit Chopper Game*; or a win and lose screen as was discussed in the same chapter. There is more you can add and, in fact, there is never a complete game; whenever you open your project, you will always find something new to add to give a better gameplay experience.

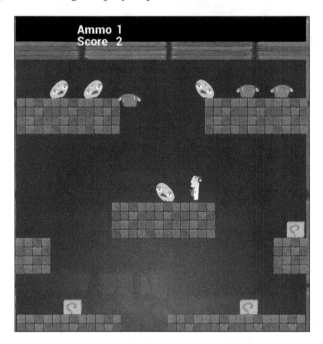

Summary

After you finished building your fourth iOS game with Unreal Engine, you have learned more about Unreal Engine. It was worth learning how to add custom inputs to your custom events, how to use the **timeline** node, how 2D colliders are optimized and why they are the best solution for 2D games, and finally a platformer on an iOS device should have virtual controllers that Unreal Engine makes possible using its unique and easy to use touch interface.

Now you have made four nice games, and it is time to move beyond the process of creating game logic and learning more about the other social and monetization features that Unreal Engine 4 provides.

7
Monetizing Your Game

Making games for mobile devices has always been tricky. As you might have seen, some games charge you money, while other games don't. However, how do those people who release their games for free make a revenue?

Monetization has always been an essential topic related to the game industry, mostly with mobile games as the mobile market has its own rules and competition. Adding ads or in-app purchases is the best way to monetize your game, but keep in mind that it has to be done in a way that makes the user like it, not in a way that makes them run away from the game.

Another thing to keep in mind is that in earlier releases, the majority of these online features were not exposed to the editor, but currently Epic has released UE 4.5, which has all the online and social features exposed in the editor, ready to be used. So I had to upgrade my system and the whole environment to UE 4.5, XCode 6.1, and OS X Yosemite to enjoy the new features and engine optimizations.

By the end of this chapter, you will be able to do the following tasks:

- Show and hide ads
- Create a game profile on iTunes
- Add features to the game profile
- Implement in-app purchases
- Enable, show, and update the leaderboard in the game
- Access the achievements system in the game

iAd support

Displaying ads in mobile games has always been one of the essential but complex topics. However, that was before Unreal Engine started supporting ads (meaning that you can add some banners inside your games to gain revenue from them), and now it has become much easier. While it is still an experimental feature inside the engine, it looks promising anyway. Currently, Epic supports iAd for iOS devices, but if you are more interested in integrating other ads services, then you will need to contact the provider, work on writing your own wrapper for it, and then compile the editor.

To show an ad banner, you just call a node named **Show Ad Banner** and you'll find that it is tagged as **EXPERIMENTAL** if you are running the older editor version. This node has only one option with a checkbox. If the **Show on Bottom of Screen** option is checked, the ad will be displayed at the bottom of the screen, otherwise it will run on the top section of the screen. Normally, these are the only two places to show an ad unless they are fullscreen ads. So, ensure that you show the ads during a game menu screen or even a cut scene.

When it comes to a gameplay session, it is better to hide the ads to avoid the player accessing them by mistake. Doing this is even easier. Epic provides two nodes to hide an ad banner. The **Force Close Ad Banner** node will totally close and terminate the ad session, and this might cause you to lose some revenue, while using the **Hide Ad Banner** node will work in hiding the banner till you call it again. As mentioned earlier, these are tagged as **EXPERIMENTAL** nodes if you are running an older editor.

iTunes Connect

You already know that using the iOS developer portal is the way to prepare your iOS game for release by building the provisioning profile, certificates, devices list, and the bundle ID. Now when the journey of creating a game comes to its end, you have to access what is called iTunes Connect.

- By accessing **https://itunesconnect.apple.com/**, you'll have a dashboard that should be hosting your apps, games, charts, reviews, revenue, downloads, and everything related to your product in the post-production stages.

- The most important part right now is **My Apps**, where you will be building the first profile for your first ready-to-go game. Because you are using ads, **In-App Purchases (IAP)**, leaderboards, or achievements, you need to create a setup inside the game profile first. Then, you can keep developing inside Unreal Engine. Once you access the **My Apps** section, you'll find that it is mostly empty, so start adding a new app using the plus icon in the top-left corner, as you must have an app dashboard to be able to have an app on the App Store.

- Fill in all the provided sections. Use the **Name** field of the game you are willing to use, set the **Primary Language**, and pick a **Bundle ID** from the ones you've already made in the iOS dev portal. Finally, add a version number (in the **Version** field) to the game and an **SKU**, which is just description text that no one except you will be able to see.

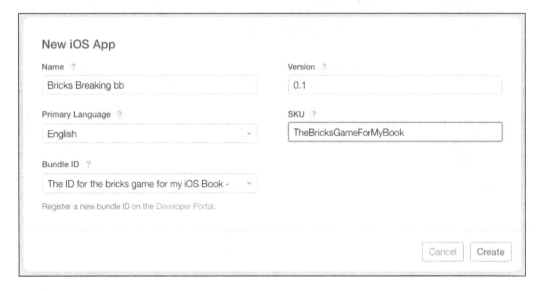

- After adding your app, you'll see its profile, which will contain tons and tons of information and requested files. Feel free to keep uploading screenshots and videos, writing descriptions, or filling some support information for your future players and users. Adding an icon is a good thing to do now.

- The most important thing right now is that you focus on two tabs only: the **In-App Purchase** tab, which is meant to take care of the items you are going to sell, and the **Game Center** tab.

- Using the **In-App Purchase** tab, you can set up a product ID to be used in the game. Feel free to read more about this part in Apple's documentation to pick the correct product types for your game.

- When you open the **Game Center** tab, you'll find that it focuses on only two things: the **Leaderboard** and **Achievements** sections. As you can see, it is very easy to keep adding items to the lists. Feel free to fill both lists with the items that your game needs. However, keep in mind that the names that you'll be using and choosing will be needed in the engine to complete the logic.

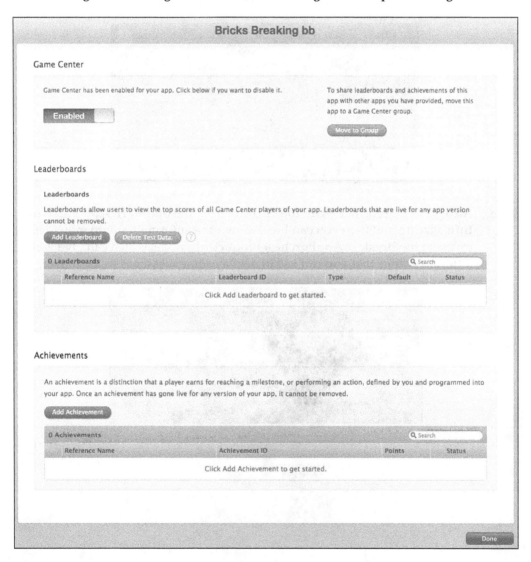

Adding in-app purchases

- To make an IAP request in an Unreal Engine game, you will need to add a single node called **Make An in-App Purchase**, assign the current player controller to it, and pass **Product Identifier** as a string from the iTunes Connect account. Then, you can make different scenarios based on the result. For example, if the player purchases a pack of in-game currency, you can add the amount of the currency to the player's profile on success or you can display an error message on the UI on failure.

- Also, you can return the IAP information from the output **In App Purchase Information** and then you can break down this information into more detail by using the **Break InAppPurchaseProductInfo** node, which can give you different strings that you can use to display some messages to the player.

- With another node called **Read in App Purchase Information**, you can pass all the product identifiers as an array string, and it will return all the information related to them. You can then use this information to display some sort of text inside the game store. This is useful if you change some information later, as this way you don't have to make an update to the game to update the store information. If the store gets its information directly from the iTunes Connect identifiers, then it will get the information once you change it. Let's say you changed the price of a product; using **Read in App Purchases Information** at the beginning of the game will ensure that the most recent test data to be displayed in the game store is returned to you.

Adding leaderboards

A leaderboard, as with any other online feature, is very simple and quick to integrate. After adding your leaderboard IDs in iTunes Connect, you will be able to write new values and update them for any of those IDs by calling the **Write Leaderboard Integer** node. Usually, passing the **Player Controller** option is essential for all the online nodes. For a leaderboard, you need to assign a value for **Stat Name**, which is the iTunes Connect ID and the integer value you want to send in the **Stat Value** slot.

- If you want to display the whole leaderboard of the game to the player, or you want to show the Game Center screen of your game to your player, then you need to use **Show Platform Specific Leaderboard Screen**. This is called **Specific** because the same node is used with Android devices to display the Google Play leaderboard screen:

- Usually, you save the leaderboard values locally in the device as an integer. However, the player will be the only person on earth who will be able to know their score as no one else can see it or access it. Let's think about the highest score of the player. What if the player used another device (device B) to play the game with their account, and then they came back to the first device (device A)? Of course, the local score will not match the final score on the Game Center. This is the reason that Epic has implemented the **Flush Leaderboards** node to download the leaderboard values and the **Read Leaderboard Integer** node to get the downloaded values. Firing these nodes during the start of the game gets you the latest values of the player on the leaderboard, which you can compare with the local ones. If it is higher than the local score, then you will need to update the local score and then save it.

Adding achievements

As leaderboards and achievements used to be discussed together as one topic, Epic has done their best to make the **Achievements** process similar to the **Leaderboard** process, which is as follows:

1. Use the **Write Achievement Progress** node.

2. Assign a value for **Achievement Name**, which represents the ID in iTunes Connect.

3. Pass a **Progress** value to it if it is a progression achievement.

4. You don't have to use a user tag, but this value will be returned anyway on success and on failure.

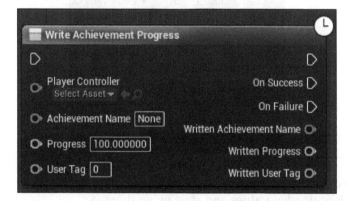

You can also use a similar node on the leaderboards to display the Game Center achievements screen by calling **Show Platform Specific Achievements Screen**. This too is named **Specific** as it is used with Android to show the Google Play **Achievements** screen.

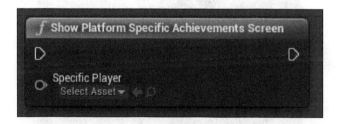

As leaderboards have the functionality to download the progress and get its values, achievements have similar functionality too. However, as an achievement has a progress and description and not just progress (unlike the leaderboard), achievements have four nodes. The **Cache Achievement** node and the **Cache Achievement Description** node both download and cache (save on the device) the achievement progress and description. So, if the player has no Internet connection and still wants to display the achievements, they still have a chance to display it offline with caching.

The **Get Cached Achievement Progress** and **Get Cached Achievement Description** nodes get the downloaded values and start using them.

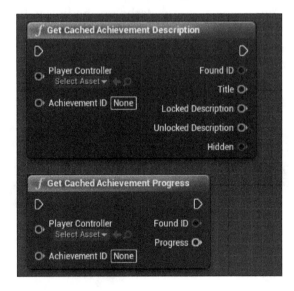

Summary

Now you've got your hands on the how and why to use ads, IAP, leaderboards, and achievements, and know how easy the hard stuff becomes when you use Unreal Engine to process them.

While you have already got the core elements of monetizing an iOS game, before you move forward to the next chapter and start optimizing your game's performance, I would suggest you read some articles on the monetization science, as showing ads or adding IAP, or even achievements are just the tools and methods to monetize, but to make a successful monetization you've got to use these features at certain points during the gameplay.

8
iOS Debugging and Optimization

Debugging has always been a strong topic when it comes to game development. With every development, there is a debugging process to help the product's performance and push it to the best, make it as bug-free as possible, and remove the performance issues. However, when it comes to games and especially mobile games, debugging is the number one priority topic as these devices are not usually powerful enough to handle some aspects of the game.

By the end of this chapter, you will:

- Learn how to use the editor in different ways to debug your games
- Understand the different ways in which XCode can help in debugging your games
- Learn how to optimize the game performance
- Learn how to minimize the game size

Blueprints Live view

What could be better than having a visual representation of the game logic during runtime! Using blueprints, you guarantee that when it comes time to find a bug, it will be a very quick process.

Being able to see the code execution process, which is something that is running in the background, but you didn't think about it. If you have a dual screen or even if you just have a big screen and you can shrink your window size, try to put the viewport alongside the blueprint view. Then by pressing the play button, you will see a visual representation with flashing red and yellow lines into and out of the nodes that are being executed right now. Like **Event Begin Play**, when the game starts, it shows you the execution of its **SET** integer node.

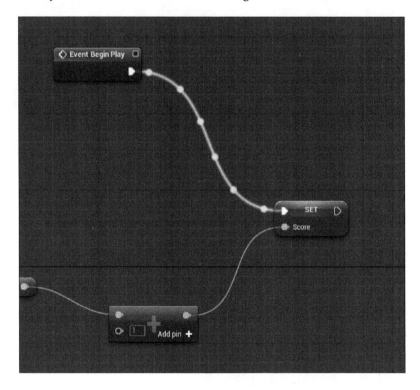

Usually, when you have a bug, it is because there is something that has not been executed or has been executed in the wrong way or with wrong values. Using this method is simple and easy. You can see if a specific node has been executed or not, and if it was executed, in which order or with what values.

Printing messages

Printing messages to the console has always been a quick and easy way to check the occurrence of a function or perhaps the changes in a variable over time. Unreal Engine has a very advanced **Print String** node. When you use the node for the first time, it appears that it'll be printing the request **In String** value to the console.

However, if you press the little down arrow at the bottom of the node, it will show you more options. These options give you the chance to print this message to the console using **Print to Log**, print to the player game view using **Print to Screen**, or even use both!

The **Text Color** option is the color of the printed text on the screen. This only works if you have selected the **Print to Screen** option; otherwise it is useless as the console always prints messages in one color—black!

To be able to see the console/log messages during your development process, the best way is to watch it through the **Output Log** window that you can access from the **Window** panel.

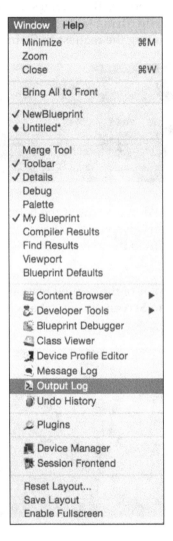

The **Output Log** screen not only prints messages from your blueprints' logic, but also prints messages from the internal engine core. It is also a good place to follow the progress of building and packaging a playable version of the game. The **Output Log** screen is a log for anything related to your Unreal Engine project—not only code and engine-related stuff, but anything else too. It is always a good place to check for the cause of crashes or building and packaging failures.

The **Output Log** window has its own tagging system, and any printed line will have a tag for itself. For example, a printed message from a **Print String** node in your blueprint will usually start with **LogBlueprintUserMessages:**.

Breakpoints

As the name implies, a breakpoint is a point where the game will be forced to break for a while. If you are from a programming background, then you definitely know what breakpoints are.

A breakpoint is something you add to your logic to ask the game/app to pause the execution process once it reaches this point. To add a breakpoint to a certain node, all that you need to do is right-click on the node itself and choose **Add Breakpoint**.

Once you finish adding the breakpoint, the node will be tagged with the breakpoint icon. However, the first time, you'll see that the breakpoint icon looks strange.

The icon shown in the preceding screenshot means that you've successfully added the breakpoint to the node. However, it will not be effective until you compile the blueprint logic. Once you compile your blueprint, the breakpoint icon will change to show the usual red icon.

Now you have a breakpoint in the game that should take place once this **Destroy Actor** node has been called. While running the game, when this node is executed, you'll find:

- The game pauses
- The blueprint opens on that node and marks it with giant red arrow
- The app shows the flow input to the current breakpoint node

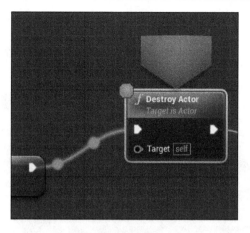

Now comes the most interesting part of debugging. By opening the **Blueprint Debugger** window from the **Window** toolbar, you will have access to the **Blueprint Debugger**.

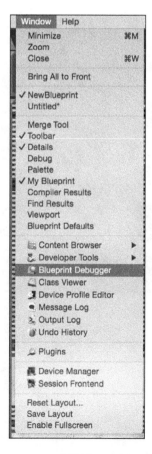

This window gives you a lot of information about the execution of the nodes and how long it takes. It also shows you an execution trace for all of the nodes and their execution order. It also shows you the nodes tagged by blueprint and you can use this window as a quick way to disable or enable breakpoints.

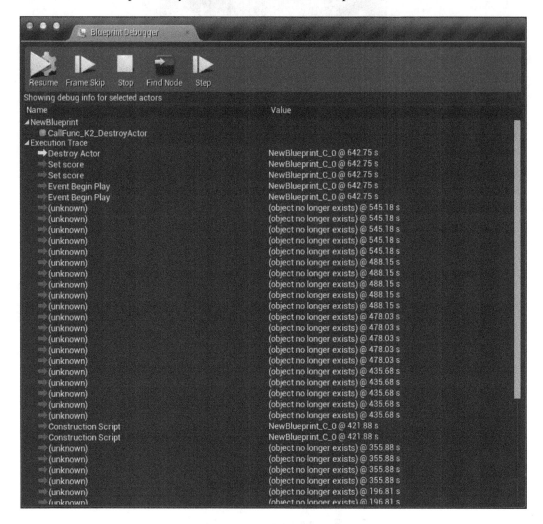

Once you find the issue, you need to get rid of the breakpoint. All that you need to do is right-click on the node again and select **Remove Breakpoint**.

You can also remove the breakpoint but keep a reference for it. Let's say this node was often a cause of different issues and you want to remember that. So you could choose **Toggle breakpoint** and make it nonfunctional, but it will still be marked as a breakpoint entity. So once you see it, you'll know that it is a switched off breakpoint that is not active right now and you can re-enable it whenever you want.

If you have lots of breakpoints, usually while tracking a very serious bug, you'll keep adding breakpoints everywhere in all of the blueprints. However, once you fix the problem and need to clean your logic of those breakpoints, it does not make any sense to open the blueprints one-by-one and manually remove them. That's the reason behind adding the **Disable All Breakpoints** and the **Delete All Breakpoints** options in the **Debug** menu. Also, once you use **Disable All Breakpoints**, the **Enable All Breakpoints** option will be enabled to give you the opportunity to reactivate all of them again if you want.

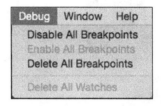

XCode tools

As long as you are developing for iOS or OS X, you must use XCode for one task at least. Although Unreal Engine can directly give you a running game in your device or a final cooked IPA, you can still run the game via XCode.

Any game that is cooked using Unreal Engine either for direct play on the device or an IPA as a result of a project generated and compiled by XCode.

To find this autogenerated project, you can just browse your Unreal Engine's project directory and find it alongside the Unreal project file. It is usually named with the same name.

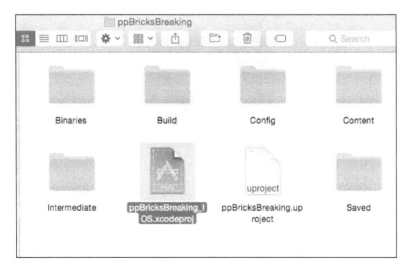

When you open this project, you will find it is set to **UE4CmdLineRun** by default. Usually, it will not run once you try to build in your device. So first you need to change the scheme to **UE4Game – iOS** and then choose your connected device from the list.

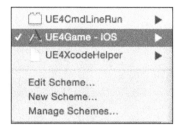

Debug Navigator

To access the debugging tools, you need to click the sixth icon on the left-hand side panel icon bar, which usually shows a **Show the Debug Navigator** tool tip, and this will give you direct access to the debugging tools.

Understand that accessing this panel without running a game on the device will show you a totally empty panel. You must have a running game on the device to start seeing the tools shown here:

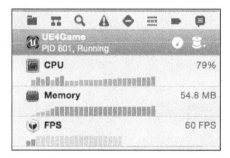

The first part called **UE4Game** has general information about the game. It is not much, but it is useful anyway. It gives you the **PID** value, which is the process ID of **601**, and the current state of this process, which is obviously **Running**.

The second row of the toolset is the **CPU**. Accessing it will show you how many threads the device is running at the moment, the performance of each thread, and the utilization of each running process. Because you are running **UE4Game**, it will be the main focus here; any other running processes on the device will be listed in **Other Processes**. The amount of free CPU capacity will be listed in **Free percentage**.

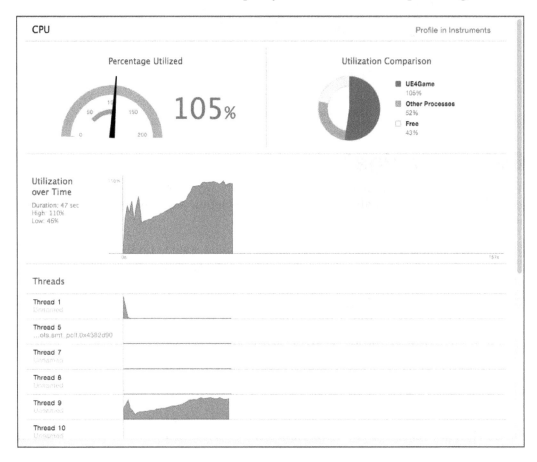

The third row is **Memory** and it looks a lot like the **CPU** tool; in fact, it works in the same way, and the only difference is that the memory tool measures the memory capacity in MB.

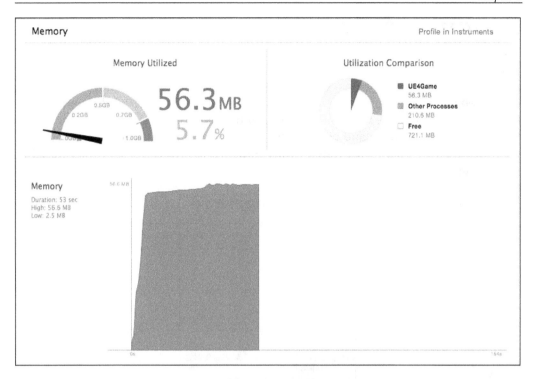

The last row is meant for the **FPS** measurement. **FPS** is short for **frames per second**. A good game should be running on 60, but since complex games usually can't reach this frame rate, 30 is a good frame rate. The highest frame rate is the best and the lowest frame time is the best as well, because a low frame time would mean a high frame rate. As you can see, the frame rate is **60** and the frame time is **6.0ms**, which means rendering the frame took 6 milliseconds from the device. This is very fast. Usually, its value would be something near 15 to 20 milliseconds for more complex games.

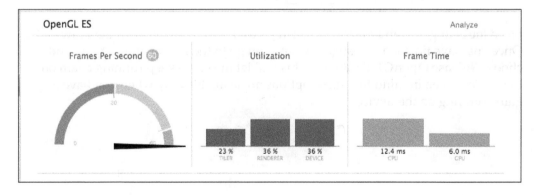

Capturing frames

You can also use the **Capture OpenGL ES Frame** option from the **Debug** menu, which will freeze the game for a while and totally change the content of the **Debug** menu to accommodate the new debugging environment. Finally, it shows you a frame debugger that contains all of the draw calls for OpenGL ES where you can see the construction and the rendering pipeline of the chosen frame. Also, you can check the used texture, shaders, and objects one by one. It is a more advanced tool, but it is very useful to use when you want to really understand how a frame gets rendered step by step.

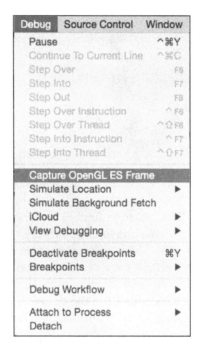

From the changed **Debug** menu, you can go back and forth between the draw calls. Once you have finished investigating, you can go to the **Debug** menu again and choose **Release OpenGL ES Frame**. This will let the game keep running again on the device. Keep in mind that these options are available only when you have a game running on the device.

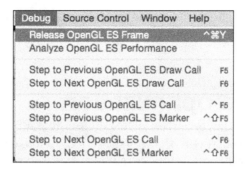

Instruments

Instruments has always been the most famous debugging tool and the most famous savior of so many games and apps for iOS and Mac OS X. As long as you are building iOS apps from OS X, you must use Instruments to check your game performance, memory leaks, allocations, system trace, and lots of other features. From the **XCode** menu, you can choose **Instruments** from the **Open Developer Tool** submenu.

Once it is open, you can choose to profile apps from different types of platforms and different types of metrics to profile. It is very easy-to-use and handy tool. Its values are very easy to read.

Performance optimization

iOS devices and mobiles in general can run games with a high frame rate, but there are some disadvantages that you need to take care of to make sure that the game will be running at its best frame rate. Here are some points that you need to check while working with Unreal games for iOS:

- Try not to use real-time lights and try to use baked lightmaps
- Make sure that you build all of the lighting before building to the device
- Pooling the actors is better than destroying and spawning them
- Don't use post process effects on the camera
- Make sure to have less than 700 draw calls in the camera view
- Use as few materials as possible to get fewer draw calls
- Use as few textures as possible; using atlases is a great way to optimize the textures' amount and size
- Square texture (power of two) is the best texture for iOS devices
- The tries count should not be more than 500,000 in the camera view
- Use **PrecomputedVisibilityVolumes** if your game has lots of 3D meshes
- Try not to use HDR or LDR if possible
- Try no to use lots of masked or translucent materials, as iOS devices are not friendly with opaque surfaces

Minimizing the game size

When it comes to packaging a game with an engine like Unreal Engine, there is not much that you can do to reduce the final installer file size, as there are so many files, headers, and things related to the engine itself that need to be shipped along with the game. Still, here are some hints that could help in reducing the final game size:

- Using less textures and game contents will guarantee that you have a smaller content folder within the IPA.
- Any unused content must have no reference. For example, if there is a testing level and it has testing content, then it needs to be removed from any logic; because any content referenced in the game will get cooked into the IPA.

- Switching the project to C++ is a great way to reduce the size a little bit, because you'll be able to disable some of the plugins such as **Slate**. Normally, the project cannot make any assumptions about which plugins and libraries you are using.

- Zipping the final IPA file before submitting to the App Store will shrink its size a little bit.

- When you make your custom **Loading** screen and game icon, save them as .png files and try to make them as simple as possible and as few as possible.

Summary

Optimizations and bug fixing are a major part of game development; in fact, what makes one logic better than another is how bug free it is. What makes a game better for a player (regardless of the game design) is how fast the game runs. Now you have got your hands on the majority of the tools and techniques the pros use to find and fix their bugs, optimize their iOS game performance, and reduce the build size.

With all of that in mind, I would recommend that you go directly to the next chapter as you will be using this bug-free optimized game with its small installer file to submit it for review to the App Store.

9
Publishing

When you have a finished and bug-free game in your hand, you still have one more step to be performed before you start working on another game or even take a couple of weeks break. This is the step where you start showing your game to the players who are waiting out there. It is the publishing and submission step.

By the end of this chapter, you will be able to:

- Package an IPA from the editor
- Change the game icon and splash screen
- Prepare the requested assets for submission
- Fill in the game information in the game dashboard
- Upload the game IPA to iTunes Connect
- Submit the game for review

Packaging the project

Before you start packaging the project and building the final IPA file, you still have one more thing to change in the game. Maybe you don't have to do it in either the editor or XCode. It is changing the game icon and splash screen. Unless you want the final game to have the default Unreal Engine logo as its icon and splash screen, you'll have to change it manually.

You can change it by replacing already built images with new ones. You can change these assets per-project or per-Unreal-Engine build. If you are working on a sequel and all of the games have to have the same splash screen and the same icon, then you don't have to waste your time and replace them every time you make a new chapter for your game.

In this case, you'll have to replace all of the images in the `Users/Shared/UnrealEngine/4.5/Engine/Build/IOS/Resources/Graphics/` directory, where all of the splash screen sizes and icons are present. Changing them in this directory means that whenever you start a new project, these will be the ones used for it. In the following screenshot, you can see the full directory of the **Graphics** folder.

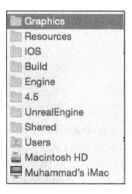

As you may have noticed, all the images look the same but each one has a different size, and this shows the reality of iOS devices having different screen sizes. Usually when you build an iOS game, it is either limited to iPad, iPhone, or both. In all cases, every device has different generations with different screen sizes, resolution, and types. Ensure that you replace all of the images, but keep their names and the PNG format as it is to avoid any errors in compilation.

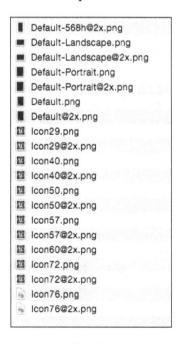

However, if you want to change these assets per project and not per engine build, which is the usual case, then you have to replace the ones that rest inside your project files and not the ones inside the Unreal Engine build. These assets can be easily found by browsing to `/ProjectName/Build/IOS/Resources/Graphics` and you may notice how easy it is to work with Unreal Engine, as all of the directories for your game project are almost the same as the directories for the editor itself.

Now, as you have already finished the only remaining step before the building step, you are ready to package the game and get the IPA out of the engine.

As you already made development and distribution provisioning profiles in *Chapter 1, Prepare to Make Unreal Games with Unreal Engine – Installing and Setting Up*, anytime you made a build, it was running as a development profile, and it was using the development provisioning profile. However, to be able to make a final build for App Store submission, you have to use the distribution profile. While you have no option in choosing which provisioning profile to use, you have the choice of the build type.

From the **File** menu, click on **Package Project,** then click on **Build Configuration**, and finally mark it as **Shipping**. You can also do it from **Packaging Settings** inside **Project Settings**. However, the **File** menu is an easy way to do it.

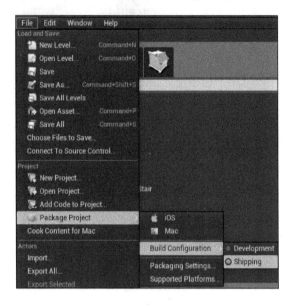

With everything in its correct place and the build type set to **Shipping**, now you have to fasten your seat belt, select **Package Project**, and select the target as **iOS**.

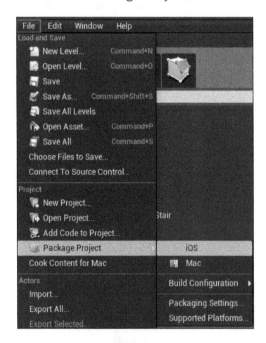

It may prompt you to ask for the packaging directory. Choosing the same directory as the project is useful.

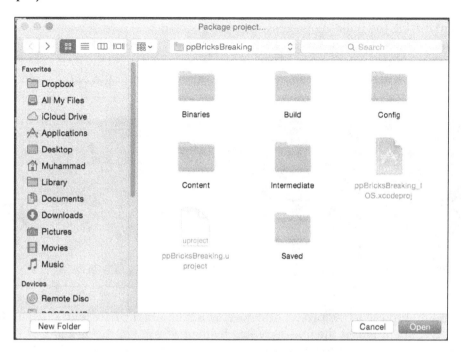

Now, the editor will show a small indicator loading and writing some information at the bottom right of the screen. You have to wait untill the process ends.

To track the progress of the packaging process, you can click the underlined **Show Output Log** text in order to display a console with a printed message for each step taking place. It will show you many messages on what exactly is done at each moment during the building process, and will also report errors or warnings while building. If everything goes right, all of the files are in the correct locations, and the certificates and provisioning profiles are correct and valid, then the project will finish correctly and will show you a success message at the bottom right of the screen and also in the output log.

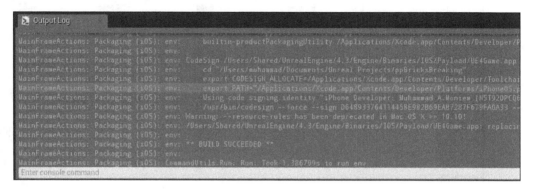

Now, if you browse to the project directory, you'll find that a new folder named **IOS** has been created. This is the folder created by the packaging process and it will hold whatever you have built so far, as long as you chose the root of the project directory as a building place.

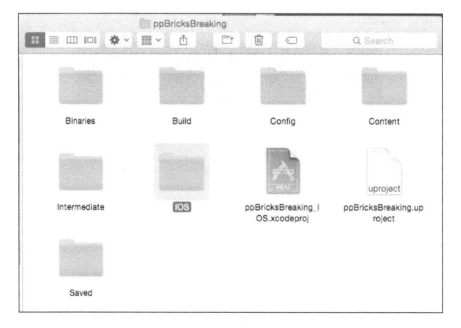

Keep in mind that the final IPA name will not affect the game's name in the App Store, as the name has already been defined in the Store itself in iTunes Connect while building the profiles for it.

The name that the packaging process will give you will be a mix of the project name, the target, and the build type. In my case, it was **ppBricksBreaking-IOS-Shipping.ipa**.

ppBricksBreaking-IOS-
Shipping.ipa

Editing the game profile

Starting from this point, all of the future publishing work will take place on the iTunes Connect website. As you already have a profile for your game from *Chapter 7, Monetizing Your Game*, you will be able to add some social stuff such as the Leaderboard and Achievements. Now you need to access this game profile again.

In the first part called **App Video Preview and Screenshots**, you can add five screenshots alongside a video for each targeted device. As you can see, Apple defines these sections by screen size, not by the device generation name. Make sure to upload the screenshots with their correct dimensions to avoid any further problems.

All of the other sections are about filling in your information, website, support e-mail, game description, the game category, the game rating, and choose to enable or disable some features such as Game Center. You need to write these things carefully as it will be the interface of your game on the App Store. Keep in mind that you can come here later and make any changes you want. Also, don't forget that any icon will be rejected if it is less than 1024*1024 pixels.

Now, on the top-right corner of the App dashboard page, the **Save** button will be highlighted, as you have already made some changes. It is a good idea to save right now. However, as you can see, the **Submit for Review** button is still grayed out, which means that there is something missing that has made the app ineligible for submission.

After saving, you'll find that the new icon has been added next to the app title, and also that there is some text indicating the current status of the app, which is currently **Prepare for Submission**.

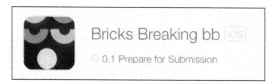

Uploading and submiting for review

As discussed in *Chapter 1, Prepare to Make Unreal Games with Unreal Engine – Installing and Setting Up*, we will use a free app called **Application Loader**. Now comes the time to use it. In fact, it is a very easy and straightforward process!

Application Loader is a free application that is meant to upload the final application binaries to Apple and ensure that the binary file fits their standards and is almost free of any bugs or errors.

After running the application loader, the first screen you see will probably be the one asking for your Apple developer account signin.

After adding the correct developer e-mail account, the application loader will ask you if you want to deliver your app or add new in-app purchases. Select **Deliver Your App** and click on the **Choose** button.

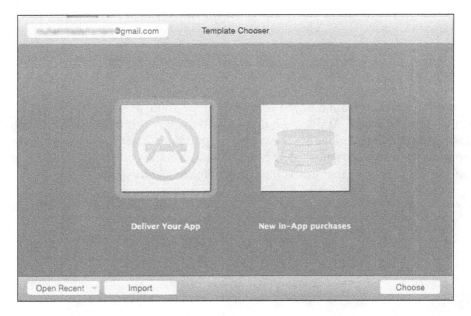

Now you need to select the final IPA file you've already packaged with Unreal Editor.

Now, you need to select the final IPA file you have already packaged with Unreal Editor.

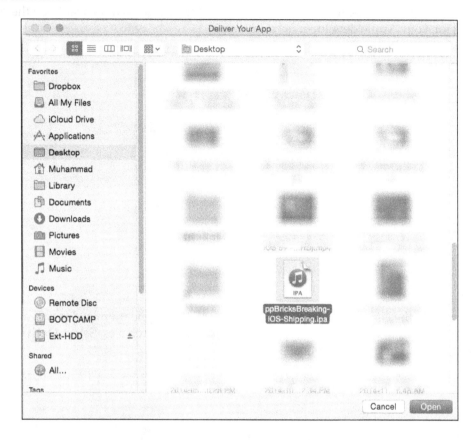

Once you have selected a valid file, Application Loader will check the binary file and get some information from it based on a real game profile that you've already created in your iTunes Connect. Application Loader will display this information as a step to ensure that you are uploading the correct app to the correct iTunes profile. By comparing the app icon, name, SKU (which is a different type of unique ID for the game), and ID, I'm sure that this is the correct binary for my game.

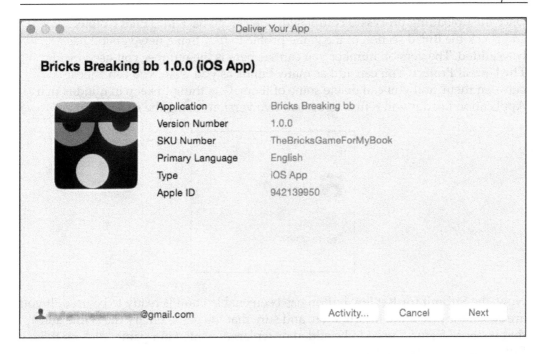

The whole process will take less than 10 minutes, and you can click on the **Activity** button to show a more detailed uploading process.

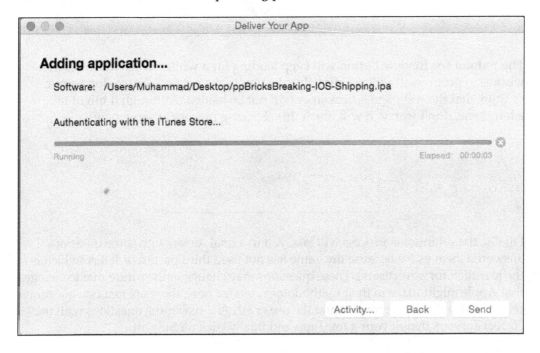

Once the uploading process is completed, you can go back to iTunes Connect and check the **Build** section of the game profile to find that a new version has been added. The version number you can see here is the number you used inside **The Unreal Project**. You can add as many builds as you wish, you can choose between them, and you can delete some of them. One thing to keep in mind is that Application Loader will refuse to upload two versions using the same number.

Now, the **Submit for Review** button has been enabled and is ready to be used. If you are sure about all of the information, and sure that the game binary file is fine and that no more features need to be added or replaced inside your game, click on the **Submit for Review** button.

The **Submit for Review** button will keep loading for a while, which indicates that work is in progress. It will not directly take you to the next screen, so don't panic or think that the webpage is broken or will not be loaded. Although it might take a long time, don't worry; it will finish this checking process at some point.

Finally, the submission process will take you to a final screen with some questions. I've answered them as **No** because my game has not used third parties or IDFA (which is the identifier for advertisers). These questions may change in the future due to changes that Apple might make in their methodology, but for now, there are just two questions related to the third-part content and the use of IDFA. Answer the questions with the correct answers that fit your game/app and finally click on **Submit**.

When the submission screen finishes loading, you will be taken back to the game dashboard screen, and you will see that the status has been changed to **Waiting For Review**.

As you can see, I've changed my version number from 1.0 to 1.2; this is because while preparing this book, I came across a new rule by Apple, according to which I had to use XCode 5.1.1 to compile the Unreal project, as 5.0 was not valid anymore. It has now become essential to use at least Xcode 5.1.1 and Application Loader 3.0. So in the future, ensure that you check the **Build** section of your game dashboard before uploading the binaries, as the rules may have changed.

After a few days, you will receive an e-mail from Apple saying that the game has passed the review, and is ready to appear on the store for the public. So if you are sure about your game, just show it to everyone. Until this moment, with the green light icon, it is approved, but still hidden from the store.

Summary

By now, you must understand what the exact steps required are to prepare for the final shipping package, and how to change the game's splash screen and icon. You also learned about most of the options on the game's dashboard of iTunes Connect, and how to upload an IPA using Application Loader and submit it for review on Apple's website. With all of this information in your pocket, I suggest you keep packaging all of the other examples you made along the course of this book and keep submitting your games to Apple; share them with your friends to show them the epic work you have done with Unreal Engine 4.x, and don't forget to recommend this book to them.

Nodes Database

In previous chapters, you've been using lots of nodes to build up the game logic. Of course, the nodes you used with the examples in this book are not all of the nodes that Unreal Engine 4 contains, but they were the most essential ones you needed to build the game logic. Some of these nodes may be changed in the future while others may be removed. However, as of now you will have this small appendix as a reference for the most common nodes used during this book. You can come here anytime to learn about the usage of a specific node you found while looking into the project files and blueprints. The most common nodes are:

- **Event Begin Play**: Anything connected to this node will start executing itself once the game starts, or once the actor is spawned into the world.

- **Event Tick**: Anything connected to this node will be executed in every frame as long as the game is running.

- **InputTouch**: This is an event node, which means that it fires itself when the event takes place. As the name implies, it will be fired when a touch action takes place. You can execute some functions when the touch is pressed or released, and this can be done using data such as the touch location or the finger index

- **Event Begin Input Touch**: This is an event node that fires itself when a touch action is initiated, and can only pass the finger index.

- **Event End Input Touch**: This is an event node that fires itself when a touch action ends, and can only pass the finger index.

- **Event Touch Enter**: This is an event node that fires itself when a touch input enters a collision area, such as the start of overlapping of a collider. This can only pass the finger index.

- **Event Touch Leave**: This is an event node that fires itself when a touch input leaves a collision area, such as completion of overlapping of a collider. This can only pass the finger index.

- **Get Dynamic Material Instance**: If the current mesh has a dynamic material, then accessing it with this node is the best way to start changing some values (such as color) of this material. The node needs a target mesh and source material as inputs.

- **Set Vector Parameter Value**: This is a node that is usually used with dynamic materials to set its parameter. It needs a target, parameter name, and a value to be set to.

- **Custom Event**: This is an empty node that represents a set of procedurals to be called. You can imagine it to be a function.

- **For Loop**: This is a typical loop to repeat some procedure until a finish point. It requires a first index to start with and a last index to stop when it hits.

- **For Loop With Break**: This is a typical loop but it has an extra input as a reason to break the loop.

- **Branch**: This is the match of an `if` statement in programming languages. It takes an input and checks whether it is `True` or `False`.

- **Random Integer in Range**: This is a mathematical node that will give a random integer value between a `Min` and `Max` value that you can enter.

- **Make Transform**: This is a node that will build a transform by using three inputs as Vector3 values. These three inputs are location, rotation, and scale.

- **Make Vector**: This is a node that works on building a Vector3 value by using three deferent float values as X, Y, and Z.

- **Break Vector**: This is a node that works on breaking a Vector3 value into three deferent float values as X, Y, and Z.

- **Set Material**: This is a node that works on setting a material into a target mesh.

- **Set Visibility**: This works on changing the current visibility state of the **Target** actor into the **New Visibility** state.

- **Play Sound at Location**: This plays a sound input at the location input.

- **Component Has Tag**: This is a comparison node to check whether the **Target** component has the **Tag** input value.

- **Actor Has Tag**: This is a comparison node to check whether the **Target** actor has the **Tag** input value.

- **Print String**: This is a node that prints the **In String** value either to the screen, to the log, or both using the **Text color** input as the text color.

- **Get Actor Location**: This is the node that gets the **Target** actor location as a Vector3 value.

- **Open Level**: This is a node that loads a new level that has **LevelName** as an input.

- **Get Player Controller**: This is a node which returns the player controller that uses **Input Player Index**. It is heavily used to return the current player, which is usually number 0 for a single player.

- **Get Hit Result Under Finger by Channel**: This gets the **Hit** result as an output of a finger press using the current player controller as a target. It has some advanced inputs such as the trace channel, which is better to be set to **Visibility** to check the visible object only.

- **Break Hit Result**: Any hit with the physics system has a result, which can be very useful to do lots of things. Any hit result can provide **Location**, **Normal**, **Impact Point**, **Impact Normal**, **Physics Material**, **Hit Actor**, **Hit Component**, and **Hit Bone Name**.

- **Enable Input**: This enables the input functionality of the current actor.

- **Get AllActors Of Class**: This is a search node that will look inside the current scene for all **Actor** class types.

- **Add PaperSpriteComponent**: This adds a new paper sprite component into the **Target** actor using the relative transform.

- **Spawn Emitter at Location**: This is a spawn node that instantiates an emitter template input into a **Location** input with a **Rotation** input using the **Auto Destroy** option.

- **Destroy Component**: This is a node that totally removes the **Target** component from the current/selected actor.

- **Destroy Actor**: This is a node that will totally remove the **Target** actor from the scene.

- **Delay**: This is a node that will work as a pause for the execution of the logic for a duration, and then keep executing using the `Complete` event.

- **Set Text**: This node usually works with the UI elements to set the text of the **Target** component into the **Value** input.

- **Set Flipbook**: This is a node meant to change the current animation clip of a **Target** animated flipbook into the **New Flipbook** value.

Index

Symbols

2D colliders
using, for advanced game 140, 141

A

achievements
adding 151, 152
advanced game
2D colliders, using 140, 141
animated sprites, building 120, 121
assets, importing 120
blueprints 121, 122
designing 119
extending 142
gameplay mechanics 122
logic, building 131
project structure 119, 120
animated sprites
building, for advanced game 120, 121
building, for Endless Runner
    Game 103, 104
animations, Endless Runner Game
idle animation 103
running animation 103
App ID
App ID Description 20
App ID Prefix 20
App ID Suffix 20
App Services 20
generating 20
Application Loader
about 181
used, for submitting iOS game
    for review 181-186

used, for uploading iOS game 181-186
using 16
App Store
game profile, preparing 16
assets
importing, for advanced game 120

B

Blender3D
using, for 3D assets 15
blueprints
about 25, 26
advantages 28
class blueprint 27
level blueprint 27
using 155, 156
blueprints, advanced game
building 123
bullet 121, 130
crateBox 121, 130
enemyGreen 121
enemyRed 121, 128, 129
gameInputs 122-125
mainChar 122, 126, 127
shootingGameMode 122, 131
spawnPoint 122, 131
uiText 122, 126
blueprints, Brick Breaking Game
ball blueprint, building 50, 60-62
bricksBreakingMode 50
building 50, 55
gameplay mechanics 51
layout blueprint, building 56-60
levelLayout 50
new level, starting 51

platform blueprint, building 50, 63
blueprints editor
  about 25
  tips and tricks 37, 38
blueprints, Endless Runner Game
  building 106
  levelLayout blueprint, building 105, 109
  madScientist blueprint, building 105, 106
  madScientistController blueprint,
      building 105, 106
  runnerMode blueprint, building 105, 108
blueprints, Fruit Chopper Game
  apple 80
  banana 80
  bomb blueprint, building 81, 90
  building 85
  fruitChopperMode 81
  fruitChopperPlayerController 81
  fruits blueprints, building 86-89
  fruitsGame 81
  kiwi 80
  LevelLogic fruitsGame blueprint,
      building 92-100
  loseScreen 81
  player controller, building 85
  watermelon 80
  win/lose blueprints, building 91, 92
  winScreen 81
breakpoints
  about 159
  adding 159-164
Brick Breaking Game
  blueprints, building 50, 55
  components, building 55
  game mode, building 52
  graphs, building 63-65
  logic, adding 63-65
  material, building 53-55
  project structure 50

C

certificates
  generating 18, 19
class blueprint 27
components, ball blueprint
  projectile movement, adding 61

projectile movement, setting 62
sphere, adding 60
components, layout blueprint
  adding 57
  billboard, adding 60
  camera, adding 57
  camera, setting 57
  static mesh, adding 58
  static mesh, setting 58

D

debugging 155
Debug Navigator
  using 165-167
devices
  adding 20
  Name option 20
  UDID option 20

E

emissive material 53
Endless Runner Game
  animated sprites, building 103, 104
  assets, importing 102
  blueprints 105
  developing 101
  extending 116
  folder structure 102
  gameplay mechanics 105
  logic, building 110-116
  project structure 102

F

frame per second (FPS) 167
frames
  capturing 168
Fruit Chopper Game
  assets, importing 78-80
  blueprints 80
  folder structure 78
  game levels 82
  gameplay mechanics 81, 82
  particles, building 82
  project structure 78

G

game
  monetizing 143
game profile
  App ID, generating 20
  certificates, generating 18, 19
  editing 179, 180
  preparing, on App Store 16
game provisioning profile
  building 39
  new project, creating 40
  *.plist file, editing 45
  project settings, editing 41-44
  setting up 39, 40
game size
  minimizing 170
GitHub version
  used, for accessing Unreal Engine 11-15
graphs, Brick Breaking Game
  ball blueprint graph, creating 70-72
  building 63-65
  layout blueprint graph, creating 66-70
  platform blueprint graph, creating 72-75

I

iAd support 144
In-App Purchases (IAP)
  about 145
  adding 148, 149
Inkscape
  using, for 2D assets 15
Instruments
  about 169
  using 169, 170
iOS game
  developing, Unreal Engine used 7
  performance optimization 170
  submitting for review, Application
      Loader used 181-186
  uploading, Application Loader
      used 181-186
iOS project
  building 45
  launching 46
  packaging 46, 47, 173-179
  pipeline 39

iTools
  using, for Windows 16
iTunes
  using, for Mac 16
iTunes Connect 145-147

K

Kismet 25

L

leaderboards
  adding 149, 150
level blueprint 27
logic, advanced game
  building 131
  building, for bullet 136
  building, for enemyRed 133, 134
  building, for mainChar 137-140
  building, for spawnPoint 134, 135
  building, for uiText 132, 133
logic, platform blueprint graph
  Actor location, defining 75
  touch state, adding 74

M

material
  building, for Brick Breaking Game 53-55
  emissive material 53
messages
  printing 157-159
monetization 143

N

nodes
  about 29, 187
  Actor Has Tag 189
  Add PaperSpriteComponent 189
  Branch 188
  Break Hit Result 189
  Break Vector 188
  Cache Achievements 33
  Cache Achievements Description 33
  Component Has Tag 189
  Custom Event 188

Delay 189
Destroy Actor 189
Destroy Component 189
Enable Input 189
Event Begin Input Touch 31, 187
Event Begin Play 187
Event End Input Touch 31, 188
Event Hit 30
Event Tick 187
Event Touch Enter 31, 188
Event Touch Leave 31, 188
EXPERIMENTAL Close Ad Banner 36
EXPERIMENTAL Show Ad Banner 35
Flush Leaderboards 32
For Loop 188
For Loop With Break 188
Get Actor Location 189
Get AllActors Of Class 189
Get Cached Achievements Description 34
Get Cached Achievements Progress 34
Get Dynamic Material Instance 188
Get Hit Result Under Finger
        by Channel 189
Get Input Motion State 36
Get Player Controller 189
InputTouch 30, 187
iOS/Mobile-only nodes 30-36
Make Transform 188
Make Vector 188
Open Level 189
Play Sound at Location 188
Print String 29, 189
Random Integer in Range 188
Read Leaderboard Integer 32
Set Flipbook 190
Set Material 188
Set Text 190
Set Vector Parameter Value 188
Set Visibility 188
Show Platform Specific Achievements
        Screen 35
Show Platform Specific Leaderboard
        Screen 33
Spawn Emitter at Location 189
Write Achievement Progress 34
Write Leaderboard Integer 32

P

particles, Fruit Chopper Game
    building 82
    material, building 82
    particle system, building 84, 85
Projectile component 49
provisioning profiles
    generating 21, 22

R

required tools
    Application Loader 16
    Blender3D, for 3D assets 15
    Inkscape, for 2D assets 15
    iTools, for Windows 16
    iTunes, for Mac 16
    preparing 15
    XCode 5.1 15

U

Unreal Engine
    about 7
    accessing, with GitHub version 11-15
    blueprints 25, 26
    building 9
    downloading, directly 9, 10
    prerequisites 8
    prerequisites, for non-Mac OS computer 8
    setting up 8
    used, for developing iOS games 7
Unreal Script 25

X

XCode
    using 164, 165
XCode 5.1
    using 15

 Thank you for buying
Learning Unreal® Engine iOS Game Development

About Packt Publishing

Packt, pronounced 'packed', published its first book, *Mastering phpMyAdmin for Effective MySQL Management*, in April 2004, and subsequently continued to specialize in publishing highly focused books on specific technologies and solutions.

Our books and publications share the experiences of your fellow IT professionals in adapting and customizing today's systems, applications, and frameworks. Our solution-based books give you the knowledge and power to customize the software and technologies you're using to get the job done. Packt books are more specific and less general than the IT books you have seen in the past. Our unique business model allows us to bring you more focused information, giving you more of what you need to know, and less of what you don't.

Packt is a modern yet unique publishing company that focuses on producing quality, cutting-edge books for communities of developers, administrators, and newbies alike. For more information, please visit our website at www.packtpub.com.

Writing for Packt

We welcome all inquiries from people who are interested in authoring. Book proposals should be sent to author@packtpub.com. If your book idea is still at an early stage and you would like to discuss it first before writing a formal book proposal, then please contact us; one of our commissioning editors will get in touch with you.

We're not just looking for published authors; if you have strong technical skills but no writing experience, our experienced editors can help you develop a writing career, or simply get some additional reward for your expertise.

PUBLISHING

Unreal Development
Kit Game
Programming with
UnrealScript

Alan Thorn

[PACKT]
VIDEO

Unreal Development Kit Game Programming with UnrealScript [Video]

ISBN: 978-1-84969-632-6   Duration: 02:23 hrs

Kick-start your career in game development with UnrealScript and the UDK

1. Step-by-step guide on how to set up the UDK and create a game with UnrealScript.

2. Explore core UnrealScript features and configurations.

3. Ideal for newcomers to UnrealScript.

iOS 7 Game Development

Develop powerful, engaging games with ready-to-use utilities
from Sprite Kit

Dmitry Volevodz   PACKT

iOS 7 Game Development

ISBN: 978-1-78355-157-6   Paperback: 120 pages

Develop powerful, engaging games with ready-to-use utilities from Sprite Kit

1. Pen your own endless runner game using Apple's new Sprite Kit framework.

2. Enhance your user experience with easy-to-use animations and particle effects using Xcode 5.

3. Utilize particle systems and create custom particle effects.

Please check **www.PacktPub.com** for information on our titles

PUBLISHING

UnrealScript Game Programming Cookbook

ISBN: 978-1-84969-556-5   Paperback: 272 pages

Discover how you can augment your game development with the power of UnrealScript

1. Create a truly unique experience within UDK using a series of powerful recipes to augment your content.

2. Discover how you can utilize the advanced functionality offered by the Unreal Engine with UnrealScript.

3. Learn how to harness the built-in AI in UDK to its full potential.

iPhone Game Blueprints

ISBN: 978-1-84969-026-3   Paperback: 358 pages

Develop amazing games, visual charts, plots, and graphics for your iPhone

1. Seven step by step game projects for you to build.

2. Cover all aspects from graphics to game ergonomics.

3. Tips and tricks for all of your iPhone programming.

Please check **www.PacktPub.com** for information on our titles

www.ingramcontent.com/pod-product-compliance
Lightning Source LLC
Chambersburg PA
CBHW060558060326
40690CB00017B/3746